ATELIER CONFECTIONERY

BONBONS, MARSHMALLOWS, TOFFEES, LOLLIPOPS, LICORICE...

YASMIN OTHMAN, PHOTOGRAPHY BY LISA LINDER

ATELIER CONFECTIONERY

BONBONS, MARSHMALLOWS, TOFFEES, LOLLIPOPS, LICORICE...

hardie grant books
MELBOURNE • LONDON

Contents

Ingredients

1 *Icing (confectioners') sugar*

This sugar has been ground into a powder. Use for making frostings and decorating cakes.

2 *Caster (superfine) sugar*

This sugar has a fine texture. Use in baking and meringues.

3 *Golden caster (superfine) sugar*

An unrefined cane sugar that is super fine. Use in baking cakes and cookies.

4 *Granulated sugar*

A coarse-grain sugar, which is also available as golden or unrefined. It is used in the making of syrups, confectionery and in everyday use, such as adding to hot drinks.

5 *Light brown sugar*

This sugar is brown in colour due to the presence and percentage of molasses. Use in making toffees and baking.

6 *Muscovado sugar*

A natural unrefined dark brown sugar with a strong flavour of molasses. It is used in making toffees and baking rich flavoured cakes.

7 *Raw (demerara) sugar*

This unrefined sugar has a light golden colour and a crunchy texture. It is used for toppings on desserts and as a sweetener in coffees.

8 ***Flavouring oils & extracts***

Oil flavourings have an intense flavour and can withstand high temperatures. Extracts are from natural products, e.g. rose petals.

9 ***Food colouring***

There are two types – pastes and liquids.

10 ***Pectin powder***

This is used as a gelling agent especially for jams and jellies.

11 ***Liquid glucose***

A thick clear sweet liquid used in the making of hard sweets.

12 ***Powdered gelatine***

This gelling agent is available as a powder or in sheets. Agar-agar flakes are vegetarian.

13 ***Vanilla pods***

The seeds are scraped out of the pod and used as a flavouring.

14 ***Dark chocolate***

The cocoa solids in dark chocolate range from 70 to 90%.

15 ***Milk chocolate***

Milk is added to dark chocolate to create milk chocolate.

16 ***White chocolate***

There are no cocoa solids but cocoa butter, sugar and milk in this chocolate.

17 ***Pink strawberry chocolate***

This is white chocolate with added flavour and colour.

Equipment

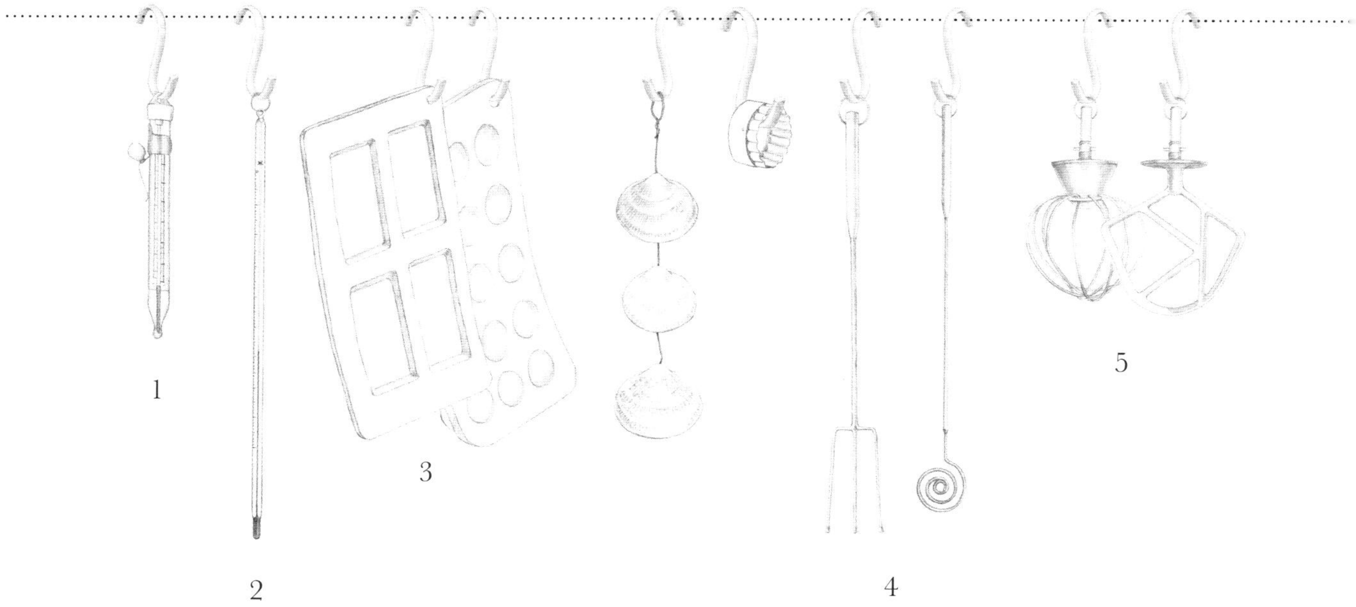

1 ***Sugar thermometer***

Essential for making sweets, jams, toffees, caramels etc. as it gives the precise temperature you need to achieve when making confectionery. It is available in different styles and as analogue or digital.

2 ***Tempering thermometer***

A must-have when working with chocolates. The thermometer is used to check the correct tempering temperature for different types of chocolate.

Heavy-based saucepans

These pans are good when cooking with sugar as they will withstand high temperatures and length of cooking time.

3 ***Candy and chocolate moulds***

These come in different materials like plastic, silicone and polycarbonate. Ensure when using a mould for boiled sweet candies that the mould can withstand high-temperature liquids.

4 ***Chocolate dipping forks***

These forks make it easy to dip candies or ganache into tempered chocolate.

5 ***Freestanding food mixer***

This is easy to use when making Italian meringues, marshmallows etc., where hot syrup is being poured in slowly.

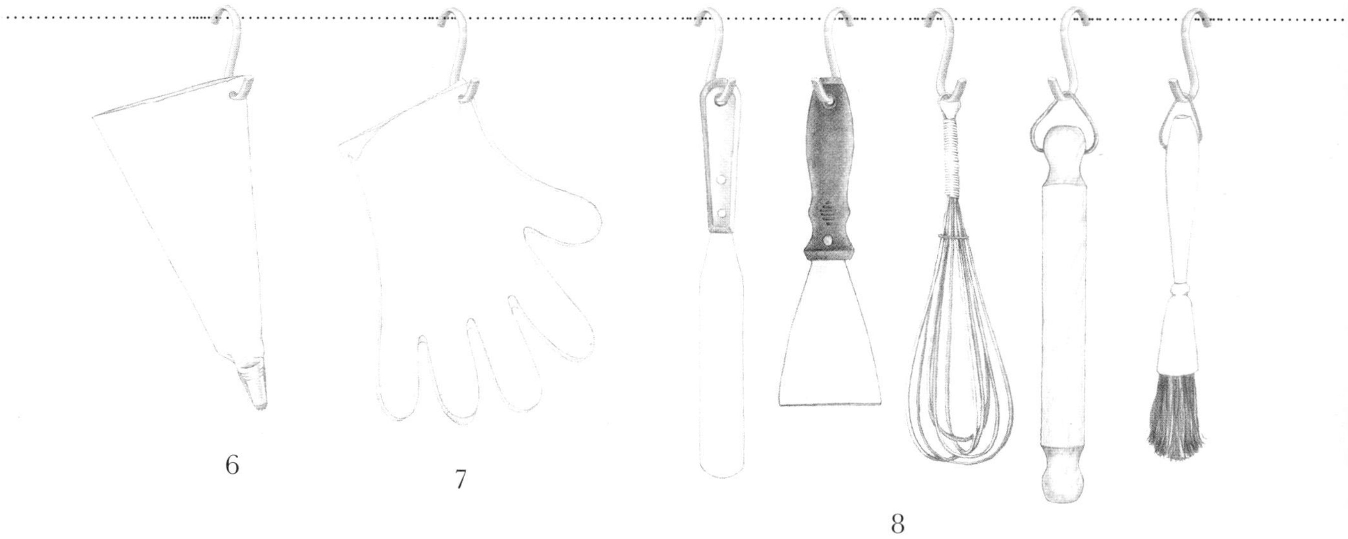

Marble slab

This is a good surface to work on to cool down sugar syrups, and to temper chocolate using the marbling technique.

Mixing bowls

Heatproof mixing bowls are ideal for melting, tempering and cooling ingredients.

6 ***Disposable piping bags***

These are very convenient. They do not need a plain nozzle to be attached as they can be snipped to however large or fine you want the tip to be.

7 ***Protective latex gloves***

These gloves are used to protect your hands from the heat of the sugar syrup when a recipe requires pulling the sugar.

8 ***Kitchen essentials***

Wooden spoons, metal spoons, spatulas, palette knives, metal scrapers, whisks, rolling pins, baking tins and trays, weighing scales, scissors, baking and greaseproof (wax) paper are also indispensable pieces of equipment that you should have on hand in the kitchen when making confectionery.

Sweets & Candies

Hard Crack Stage

149–154°C

(300–309°F)

1 Place the sugar and water in a heavy-based saucepan.

2 Heat for 5–10 minutes until the sugar has dissolved.

3 Place a sugar thermometer into the saucepan and boil the mixture.

4 If the sugar is crystallising around the saucepan, clean around the sides of the pan with a damp pastry brush to avoid any crystallisation forming.

5 Once the sugar syrup has reached the correct temperature, it has reached the hard crack stage.

6 To check that it has reached this stage, drop a little of the sugar syrup into a bowl of cold water – the sugar syrup turns hard almost immediately with brittle threads that crack or break easily.

1
2
3
4
5
6

Boiled Sweets

Tangy Apple, Wild Strawberry, Tropical Pineapple

preparation time : 10 minutes
cook time : 50–60 minutes, plus cooling

TOOLS :

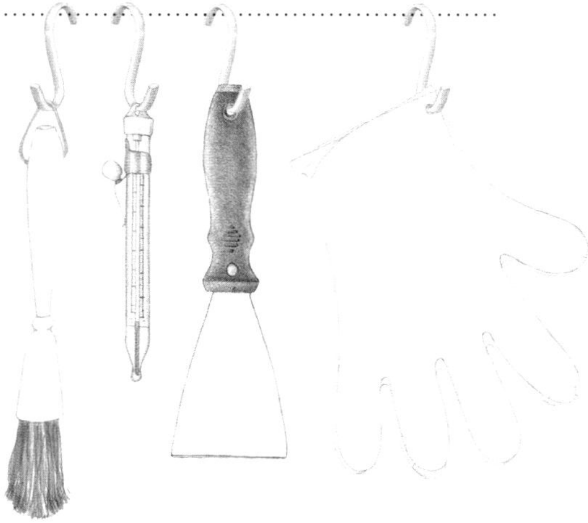

400 g (14 oz) granulated sugar
250 ml ($8\frac{1}{2}$ fl oz/1 cup) water
140 ml ($4\frac{1}{2}$ fl oz) liquid glucose
2 teaspoons citric acid (optional)
Small amount of food colouring paste (green, red, yellow)
1–2 teaspoons oil flavouring (apple, strawberry, pineapple)
Vegetable oil for oiling
Icing (confectioners') sugar for dusting

makes
45–50
pieces

• Heat the sugar, water and liquid glucose in a heavy-based saucepan over a medium heat and stir to dissolve the sugar, about 5–10 minutes.

• Insert a sugar thermometer and bring the sugar syrup to the boil, cleaning the sides of the saucepan with a damp pastry brush to avoid crystallisation around the saucepan, if necessary. Boil the mixture for 45–50 minutes until it reaches 149°C (300°F), hard crack stage.

• Once the syrup has reached the correct temperature, remove the pan from the heat and leave to settle. Add the citric acid then divide the mixture into 3 bowls. Add the different food colourings and flavourings to each bowl and stir well.

• Leave to cool slightly then pour each of the coloured mixtures, one at a time, onto an oiled marble slab. Using an oiled metal scraper or palette knife, start pushing the outer edges of the mixture inwards and working the sugar to cool it down.

• When the sugar is cool enough to handle, after about 5 minutes, wearing gloves, mould the sugar mixture into long 30 cm (12 in) ropes. If the sugar hardens too quickly, use a heat lamp or hairdryer to warm and soften the sugar mixture to make it pliable.

• Cut the ropes into 1 cm ($\frac{1}{2}$ in) pieces and leave to cool completely for about 20–30 minutes.

• Lightly dust with icing sugar and store in an airtight container in a cool dry place for 4–6 weeks.

Blackcurrant Lollipops

preparation time : 10 minutes
cook time : 50–60 minutes, plus cooling

TOOLS

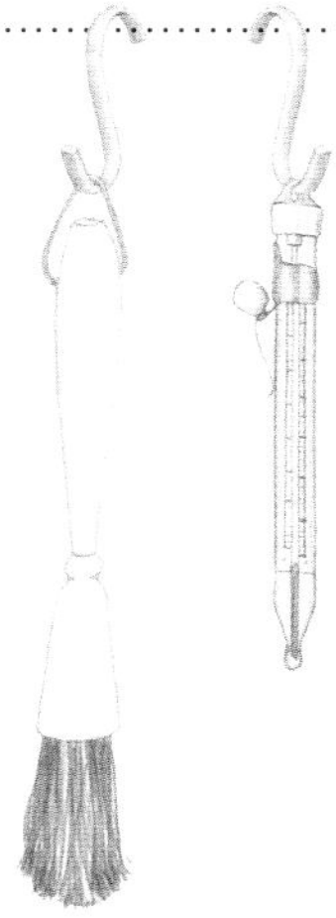

Vegetable oil spray for oiling (optional)
200 g (7 oz) granulated sugar
150 ml (5 fl oz) blackcurrant juice
60 ml (2 fl oz/¼ cup) liquid glucose
Juice of 1 lemon
Small amount of violet food colouring

makes
15
lollipops

• Line a baking tray with baking paper or lightly spray some oil into a lollipop mould and place the sticks in the mould.

• Heat the sugar, blackcurrant juice, liquid glucose and lemon juice in a saucepan over a medium heat.

• Insert a sugar thermometer and bring the mixture to the boil, cleaning the sides of the saucepan with a damp pastry brush to avoid crystallisation around the saucepan if necessary. Boil without stirring until it reaches 149°C (300°F), hard crack stage.

• Once the sugar syrup has reached the correct temperature, remove the pan from the heat and leave to settle. Add the colouring and stir well.

• Carefully pour the sugar mixture into a heatproof pitcher then slowly pour a small amount of the mixture onto the prepared baking tray to make discs. Place lollipop sticks into the discs. If using a lollipop mould, slowly pour the mixture into the lollipop mould ensuring that the sticks are covered. Leave to cool completely for about 30 minutes.

• Once the lollipops have hardened, remove from the mould and wrap in cellophane or greaseproof (wax) paper or place in an airtight container in a cool dry place for up to 2 weeks.

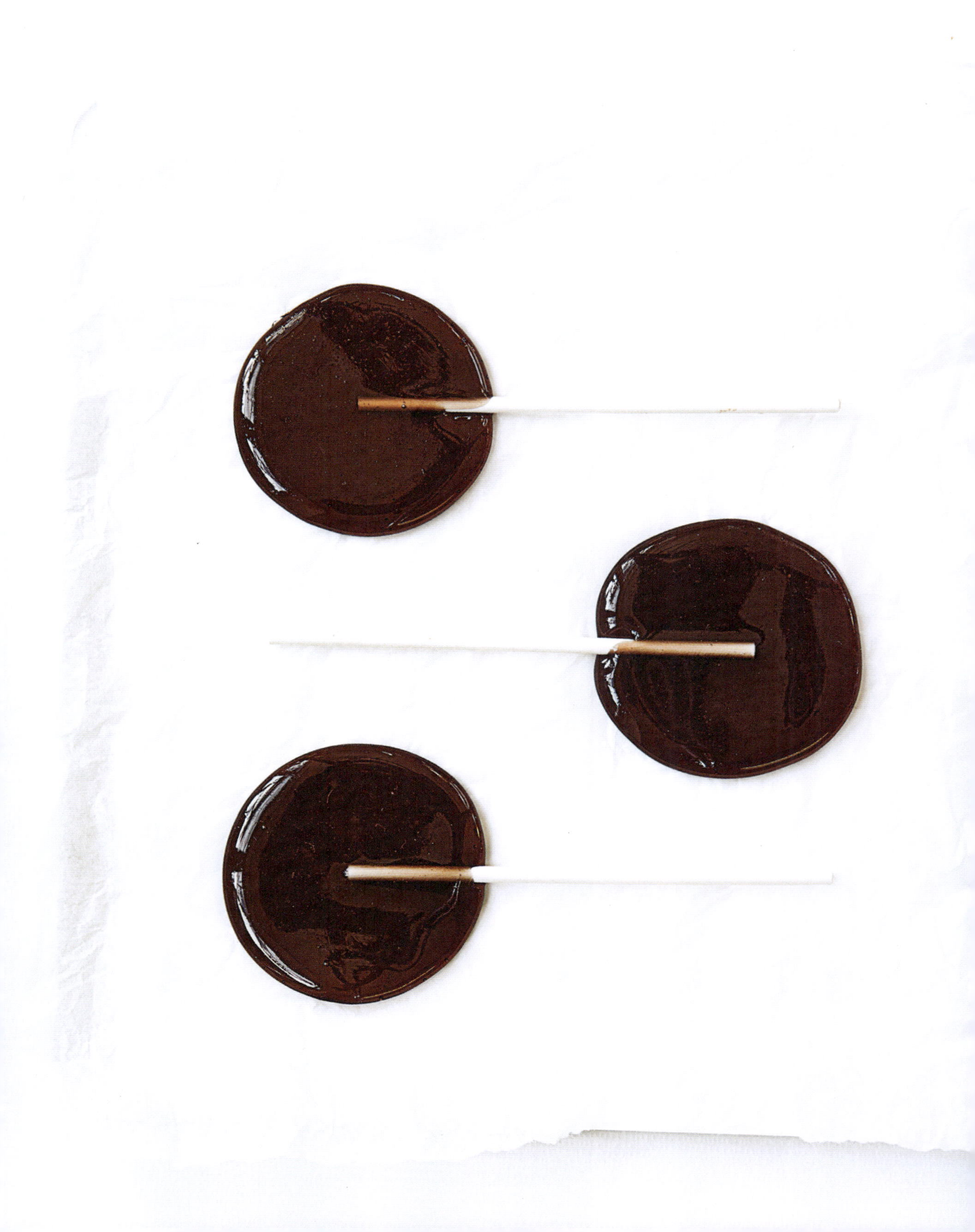

Betise

de Cambrai

preparation time : 10 minutes
cook time : 50–60 minutes, plus cooling

200 g (7 oz) granulated sugar
125 ml (4 fl oz/½ cup) water
70 ml (2¼ fl oz) liquid glucose
½ teaspoon bicarbonate of soda (baking soda)
1 teaspoon mint flavouring
Vegetable oil for oiling

TOOLS:

CARAMEL
100 g (3½ oz) granulated sugar
40 ml (1¼ fl oz) golden syrup (corn syrup)
30 ml (1 fl oz) water

makes
300 g
(10½ oz)

• Heat the 200 g (7 oz) sugar, water and liquid glucose in a heavy-based saucepan over a medium heat. Bring the mixture to the boil, then insert a sugar thermometer, cleaning the sides of the saucepan with a damp pastry brush to avoid crystallisation around the saucepan if necessary, and boil without stirring until it reaches 149°C (300°F), hard crack stage.

• Once the sugar syrup has reached the correct temperature, remove from the heat and add the bicarbonate of soda and mint flavouring. Stir well.

• Pour the mixture onto an oiled marble slab and work it by using an oiled metal scraper or palette knife, pushing the outer edges of the mixture inwards and at the same time cooling and thickening the mixture.

• Meanwhile, mould the mint-flavoured opaque mixture into a long rope about 1.5 cm (½ in) in diameter. Cut the rope into pieces and cool for 30 minutes.

• Make the caramel. Gently boil the sugar, golden syrup and water in another pan until it becomes a caramel at 160°C (320°F).

• Once the caramel is ready, remove from the heat and place the pan in a bowl of cold water to stop the caramel from cooking. Pour the caramel onto an oiled marble slab and, when it is cool enough to handle, roll into a long thin rope and, while still pliable, wrap around the mint sweets, pulling and winding the caramel around the mint.

• Cool completely for 30 minutes before wrapping or storing in an airtight container. Store in a cool dry place for up to 2 weeks.

Roudoudou

preparation time : 10 minutes
cook time : 45–50 minutes, plus cooling

TOOLS:

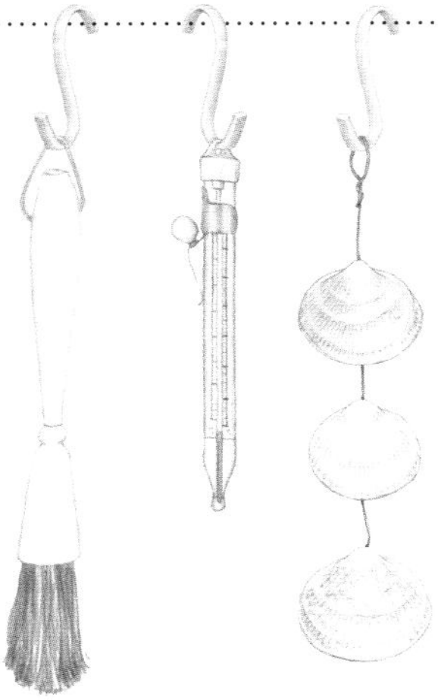

10–20 cleaned dried sea shells or plastic sea shells
200 g (7 oz) granulated sugar
125 ml (4 fl oz/½ cup) water
70 ml (2¼ fl oz) liquid glucose
1 teaspoon vanilla extract
20 g (¾ oz) butter, softened
Small amount of assorted food colouring paste

makes
10–20
pieces

• Place the clean dried shells on a large tray or use plastic coloured shells. Ensure that you use sea shells that are specifically for cooking, available from online sea shell specialists.

• Heat the sugar, water and liquid glucose in a heavy-based saucepan over a medium heat and stir to dissolve the sugar.

• Insert a sugar thermometer, bring the mixture to the boil, cleaning the sides of the saucepan with a damp pastry brush to avoid crystallisation around the saucepan, if necessary. Boil without stirring until it reaches 149°C (300°F), hard crack stage. Remove the saucepan from the heat and leave to settle, then add the vanilla extract and butter. Stir to combine.

• Divide the mixture equally among 3 heatproof pitchers, add the food colourings and mix well.

• Pour the syrup mixture into the prepared shells and leave to cool for about 30 minutes until completely cooled and hardened. Store in an airtight container in a cool dry place for up to 2 weeks.

Espresso Candy

preparation time : 5 minutes
cook time : 45–50 minutes, plus cooling

Vegetable oil for spraying
200 g (7 oz) granulated sugar
125 ml (4 fl oz/½ cup) water
70 ml (2¼ fl oz) liquid glucose
2 teaspoons coffee extract

TOOLS:

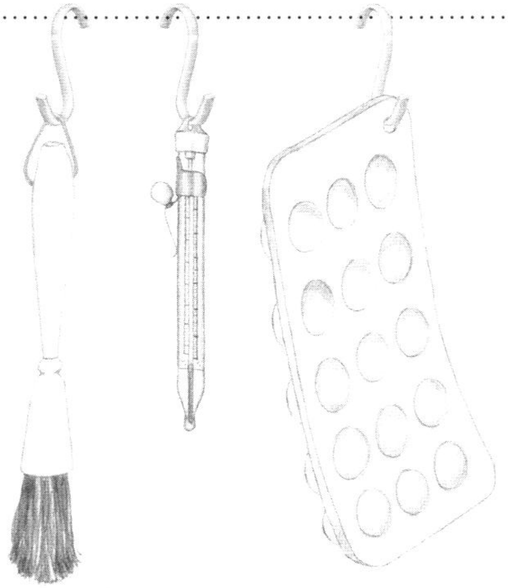

makes
100
pieces

• Lightly spray a coffee bean candy mould with some oil.

• Heat the sugar, water and liquid glucose in a heavy-based saucepan over a medium heat and stir until the sugar has dissolved.

• Insert a sugar thermometer and bring the mixture to the boil, cleaning the sides of the saucepan with a damp pastry brush to avoid crystallisation around the saucepan if necessary. Boil without stirring until the sugar syrup reaches 149°C (300°F), hard crack stage.

• Once the sugar syrup has reached the correct temperature, remove the pan from the heat and leave to settle before adding the coffee extract. Mix well.

• Pour the mixture into a pitcher, then pour the mixture into the prepared candy mould. Leave to cool for about 30 minutes until completely cold and hardened. Store in an airtight container for up to 2 weeks.

Tangerine Lollipops
with Sherbet

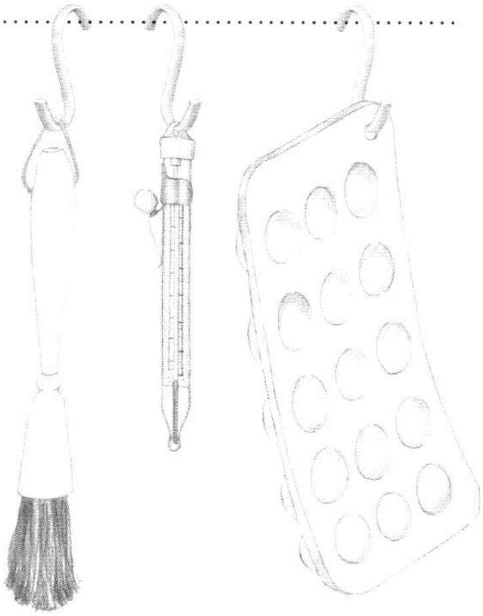

preparation time : 10 minutes
cook time : 45–50 minutes, plus cooling

TOOLS:

Vegetable oil for oiling
200 g (7 oz) granulated sugar
125 ml (4 fl oz/½ cup) water
70 ml (2¼ fl oz) golden syrup (corn syrup)
Juice of 1 lemon
½ teaspoon tangerine oil flavouring
Small amount of orange food colouring paste

FOR THE SHERBET
20 g (¾ oz) icing (confectioners') sugar
1 teaspoon bicarbonate of soda (baking soda)
1 teaspoon citric acid
8 g (¼ oz) orange flavoured jelly crystals

makes
15–20
lollipops

- Lightly spray 15–20 mini heart-shaped silicone moulds or any desired shaped moulds with some oil.
- Heat the sugar, water, golden syrup and lemon juice in a heavy-based saucepan over a medium heat and stir to dissolve the sugar.
- Insert a sugar thermometer and bring the mixture to the boil, cleaning the sides of the saucepan with a damp pastry brush to avoid crystallisation around the saucepan if necessary. Boil without stirring until the sugar syrup reaches 149°C (300°F), hard crack stage.
- Once the sugar syrup has reached the correct temperature, remove the pan from the heat and leave to settle. Add the flavouring and colouring and mix well to combine.
- Pour the mixture into a pitcher then pour into the prepared moulds. Leave to cool, inserting lollipop sticks into the sugar after 10 minutes.
- Leave to cool for about 30 minutes until completely cold and hardened. Remove from the mould and store in an airtight container in a dry place for up to 2 weeks.
- To make the sherbet, place the icing sugar, bicarbonate of soda, citric acid and jelly crystals in a small bowl and mix well to combine. Keep the mixture in an airtight container in a dry place. Serve the lollipops with the sherbet.

Honeycomb

preparation time : 5 minutes
cook time : 15 minutes, plus cooling and setting (optional)

Vegetable oil for oiling
200 g (7 oz) granulated sugar
100 ml (3½ fl oz) golden syrup (corn syrup)
2 teaspoons bicarbonate of soda (baking soda)
100 g (3½ oz) dark or milk chocolate chips (70% cocoa solids), melted and tempered (see pages 126–9), optional

makes
250 g
(9 oz)

• Line and oil a 19 cm (7½ in) square baking tin with baking paper.

• Heat the sugar and golden syrup in a large heavy-based saucepan over a medium heat until the mixture turns an amber golden colour. Remove the pan from the heat and stir in the bicarbonate of soda. The mixture will foam up.

• Pour the mixture into the prepared tin and leave to cool for about 30 minutes. Once cooled, break into shards. If using chocolate, dip one end of the shards into the chocolate and leave to set on some baking paper for at least 1 hour in a cool dry place. Store in an airtight container in a dry place for up to 2 weeks.

Cotton Candy

preparation time : 5 minutes
cook time : 45–50 minutes, plus cooling

TOOLS:

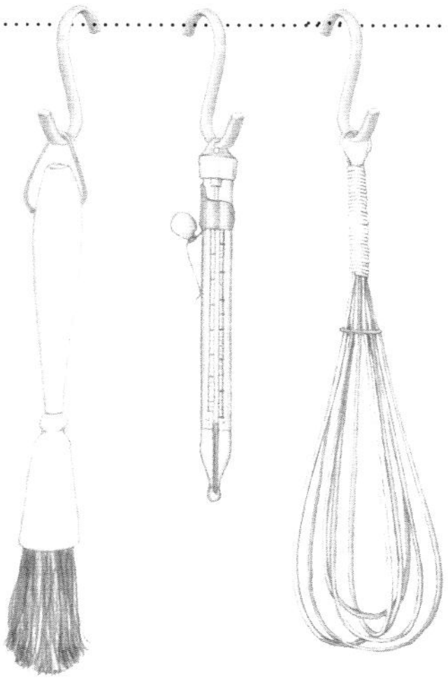

400 g (14 oz) granulated sugar
125 ml (4 fl oz/½ cup) water
125 ml (4 fl oz/½ cup) liquid glucose
2 teaspoons vanilla extract
Small amount of food colouring paste

makes
4 *large or* 8 *small*

• Prepare a whisk by decapitating it, then cut the rounded bottom of the whisk to resemble a spiky fork.

• Heat the sugar, water and liquid glucose in a heavy-based saucepan over a medium heat. Insert a sugar thermometer and bring the mixture to the boil, cleaning the sides of the saucepan with a damp pastry brush to avoid crystallisation around the saucepan if necessary. Boil the syrup without stirring until it reaches 149°C (300°F), hard crack stage.

• Once the sugar syrup has reached the correct temperature, remove the pan from the heat and leave to settle. Add the vanilla extract and food colouring and mix well. Leave to cool down slightly.

• Prepare your work surface with a large sheet of baking paper and cover the floor with some used newspaper to prevent the sugar syrup from spilling onto the floor.

• Once the sugar has cooled and thickened, dip the whisk into it and let the excess sugar drip back down into the saucepan. Move the whisk over to the baking paper and, from a height, swing the whisk back and forth so that thin strands of sugar drop onto the baking paper.

• Repeat this until you have enough spun sugar to form a nest, then insert a lollipop stick, about 8–10 cm (3¼–4 in) into the spun sugar nest, and eat immediately.

2

Toffees

Soft Crack Stage

132–143°C

(270–289°F)

1 Place the sugar and water in a heavy-based saucepan.

2 Heat for 5–10 minutes until the sugar has dissolved.

3 Place a sugar thermometer into the saucepan and boil the mixture.

4 If the sugar is crystallising around the saucepan, clean around the sides of the saucepan with a damp pastry brush to prevent this.

5 Once the sugar syrup reaches the correct temperature, it has reached the soft crack stage.

6 To check it has reached this stage, drop a little of the sugar syrup into a bowl of cold water – the sugar will turn hard with threads that will break when flexed.

1
2
3
4
5
6

Basic Toffee

preparation time : 5 minutes
cook time : 30–40 minutes, plus cooling

250 g (9 oz) soft brown sugar
70 ml (2¼ fl oz) golden syrup (corn syrup)
25 g (1 oz) unsalted butter
1 teaspoon vanilla extract
⅛ teaspoon bicarbonate of soda (baking soda)

TOOLS:

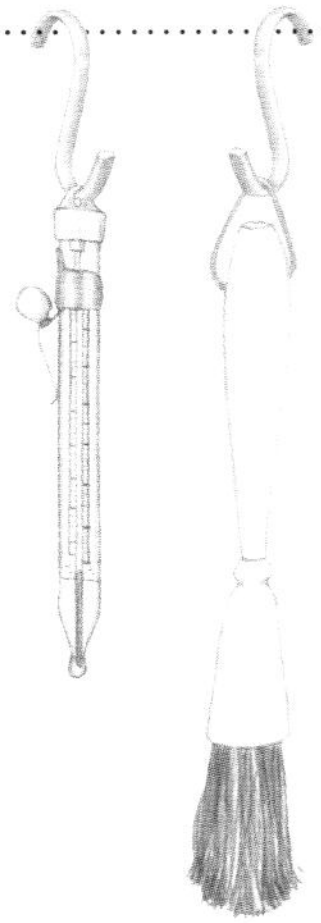

makes
300 g
(10½ oz)

• Line the base and sides of a baking tin with baking paper.

• Heat the sugar, golden syrup, butter and vanilla extract in a heavy-based saucepan over a medium heat and stir to dissolve the sugar, about 5–10 minutes. Insert a sugar thermometer and bring the mixture to the boil. Let the sugar syrup boil until it reaches 138°C (280°F), soft crack stage.

• Once the sugar syrup has reached the correct temperature, remove the pan from the heat, add the bicarbonate of soda and mix well. Pour into the prepared tin.

• When the mixture has cooled slightly, make indentations or score the top into rectangles or strips so that the toffee can easily be broken into pieces when it has cooled completely, then leave to cool for about 30 minutes, or until cold.

• When the toffee is cold, break it into pieces or shards. Store in an airtight container in a cool dry place for up to 3 weeks.

Coconut Milk & Muscovado Toffee

preparation time : 5 minutes
cook time : 40–50 minutes, plus cooling

TOOLS:

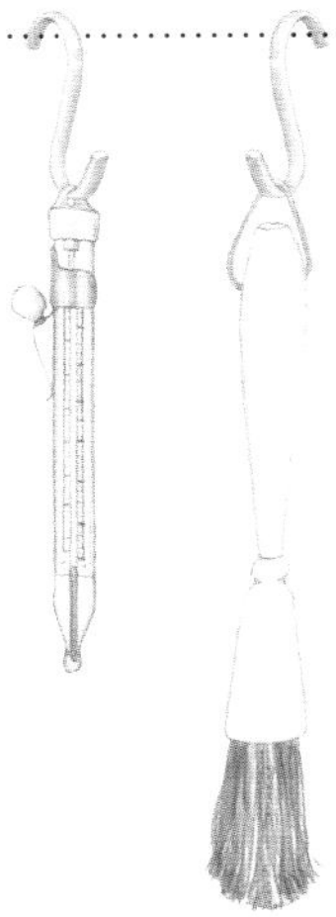

300 g (10½ oz) muscovado sugar
80 ml (2½ fl oz/ ⅓ cup) golden syrup (corn syrup)
50 ml (1¾ fl oz) coconut milk
50 ml (1¾ fl oz) thick (double/heavy) cream
30 g (1 oz) unsalted butter
1 teaspoon coconut extract
⅛ teaspoon bicarbonate of soda (baking soda)

makes
50
pieces

• Line the base and side of a baking tin with baking paper.

• Heat the sugar, golden syrup, coconut milk, cream and butter in a heavy-based saucepan over a medium heat and stir until the sugar has dissolved. Insert a sugar thermometer and bring the mixture to the boil. Let the sugar syrup boil until it reaches 138°C (280°F), soft crack stage.

• Once the sugar syrup has reached the correct temperature, remove the pan from the heat, add the coconut extract and bicarbonate of soda and mix well. Pour into the prepared tin.

• After about 5 minutes, when the mixture has cooled slightly but is still warm, snip the toffee into 1 cm (½ in) strips using a pair of scissors, then snip into 3 cm (1¼ in) lengths and, using your hands, mould the mixture into rectangular-shaped toffees.

• Leave the toffee to cool for about 30 minutes until completely cold before wrapping in cellophane. Store in an airtight container in a cool dry place for up to 4 weeks.

Pecan & Maple Toffee

preparation time : 10 minutes
cook time : 30–40 minutes, plus cooling

TOOLS:

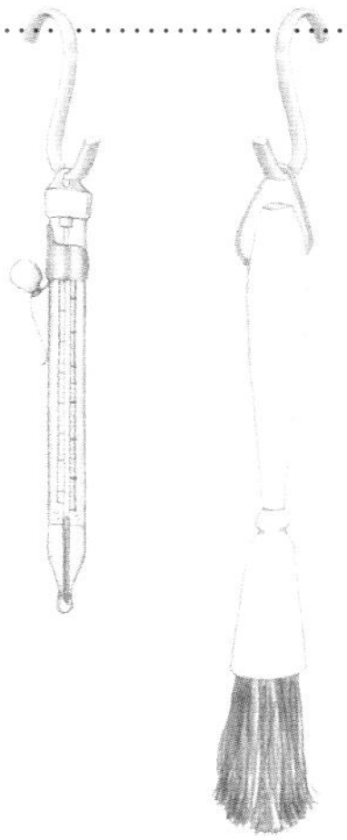

65 g ($2^{1}/_{4}$ oz/$^{2}/_{3}$ cup) pecans
190 g ($6^{1}/_{2}$ oz) soft brown sugar
70 ml ($2^{1}/_{4}$ fl oz) golden syrup (corn syrup)
30 ml (1 fl oz) maple syrup
115 g (4 oz) unsalted butter
1 teaspoon vanilla extract
1 teaspoon bicarbonate of soda (baking soda)

makes
16–20
pieces

• Line the base and sides of a 23 × 16 cm (9 × $6^{1}/_{4}$ in) baking tray with baking paper. Toast the pecans in a frying pan, leave them to cool for 5 minutes then roughly chop.

• Heat the brown sugar, golden syrup, maple syrup, butter and vanilla extract in a heavy-based saucepan over a medium heat and stir until the sugar has dissolved. Insert a sugar thermometer and bring the mixture to the boil. Let the sugar syrup boil until it reaches 138°C (280°F), soft crack stage.

• Remove the pan from the heat, add the pecans and bicarbonate of soda then mix well and pour into the prepared tin.

• Leave the toffee mixture until it is cool enough to handle, but still warm, then score indentation lines to make 5 × 4 cm (2 × $1^{1}/_{2}$ in) squares or rectangles. Leave to cool for about 30 minutes until completely cold, then break into pieces.

• Wrap each toffee in greaseproof (wax) paper and store in an airtight container in a cool dry place for up to 4 weeks.

3

Caramels

Hard Ball Stage

121–129°C

(250–264°F)

1 Place the sugar and water in a heavy-based saucepan.

2 Heat for 5–10 minutes until the sugar has dissolved.

3 Place a sugar thermometer into the saucepan and boil the mixture.

4 If the sugar is crystallising around the saucepan, clean around the sides of the saucepan with a damp pastry brush to prevent this.

5 Once the sugar syrup reaches the correct temperature, it has reached the hard ball stage.

6 To check it has reached this stage, drop a little of the sugar syrup into a bowl of cold water – the sugar syrup turns into a hard ball but can still be squeezed.

1

2

3

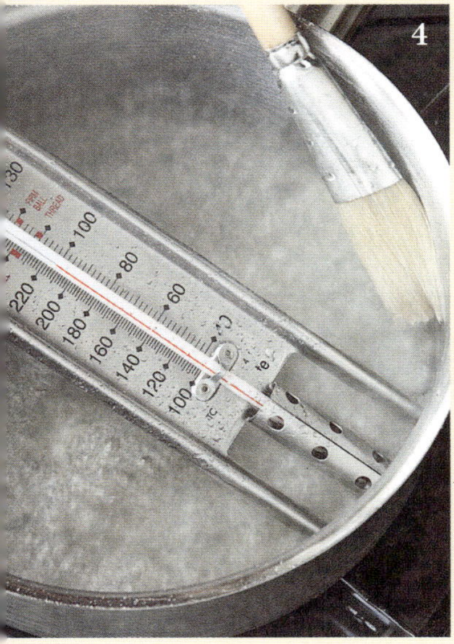
4

5

6

Caramel Candy

preparation time : 10 minutes
cook time : 20–25 minutes, plus setting

TOOLS:

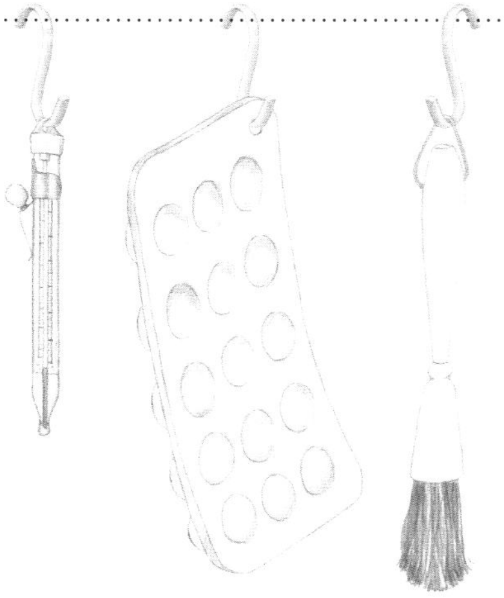

Vegetable oil for oiling
250 g (9 oz) granulated sugar
125 ml (4 fl oz/½ cup) thick (double/heavy) cream
1 tablespoon golden syrup (corn syrup)
30 g (1 oz) unsalted butter, cut into cubes
Seeds from 1 vanilla pod

makes 25–30 *pieces*

- Lightly oil a candy mould or line the base and sides of a 27 × 18 cm (10¾ × 7 in) baking tray with baking paper.
- Heat the sugar, cream, golden syrup and butter in a heavy-based saucepan over a medium heat and stir until the sugar has dissolved. Insert a sugar thermometer and bring the mixture to the boil. Boil the caramel mixture until it reaches 125°C (257°F), hard ball stage.
- Remove the pan from the heat and add the vanilla seeds, then stir until well combined. Pour the caramel into the prepared mould or baking tray and leave to set for about 20–30 minutes until firm.
- Once set, unmould or remove from the baking tray and cut into 4 × 4 cm (1½ × 1½ in) pieces on a chopping board. Wrap in greaseproof (wax) paper and store in an airtight container in a cool dry place for up to a week.

Carambars

preparation time : 5 minutes
cook time : 20–30 minutes, plus setting

TOOLS:

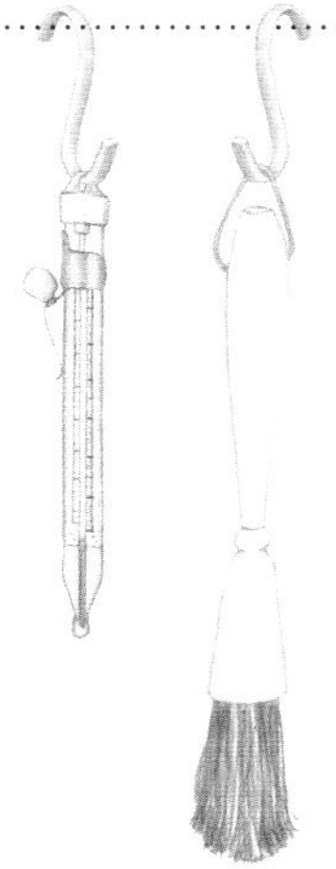

250 g (9 oz) granulated sugar
60 ml (2 fl oz/¼ cup) water
190 ml (6½ fl oz/¾ cup) condensed milk
170 ml (5½ fl oz/⅔ cup) golden syrup (corn syrup)
80 g (2¾ oz) unsalted butter, cubed
70 g (2½ oz) dark chocolate (at least 70% cocoa solids), finely chopped

makes
90
pieces

• Line the base and sides of a 27 × 18 cm (10¾ × 7 in) baking tray with baking paper.

• Heat the sugar, water, condensed milk, golden syrup and butter in a heavy-based saucepan over a medium heat and stir until the sugar has dissolved. Bring the mixture to the boil, add the chocolate, insert a sugar thermometer and cook the caramel mixture until it reaches 125°C (257°F), hard ball stage.

• Once the chocolate caramel has reached the correct temperature remove the pan from the heat and pour onto the prepared tray. Leave the caramel to set for about 30–45 minutes, or until firm.

• Once the caramel is firm enough to cut, remove it from the tray and cut into 9 cm (3½ in) lengths and 1 cm (½ in) widths. Wrap in greaseproof (wax) paper and store in an airtight container in a cool dry place for up to a week.

Fleur de Sel
Caramels

preparation time : 5 minutes
cook time : 20–25 minutes, plus setting

TOOLS:

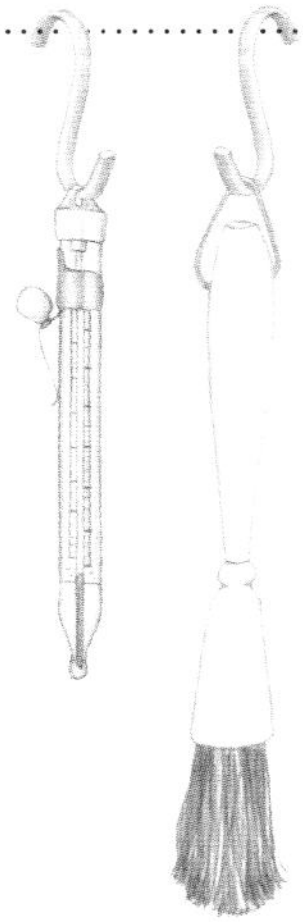

250 g (9 oz) granulated sugar
125 ml (4 fl oz/½ cup) thick (double/heavy) cream
1 tablespoon golden syrup (corn syrup)
30 g (1 oz) unsalted butter, cubed
2½ teaspoons fleur de sel
Seeds from 1 vanilla pod

makes
60–70
pieces

• Line the base and sides of a 19 cm (7½ in) square baking tin with baking paper.

• Heat the sugar, cream, golden syrup and butter in a heavy-based saucepan over a medium heat and stir until the sugar has dissolved. Bring the mixture to the boil, insert a sugar thermometer and cook the caramel mixture until it reaches 125°C (257°F), hard ball stage.

• Remove the pan from the heat and add 1 teaspoon of the fleur de sel and the vanilla seeds. Stir until well combined.

• Pour the caramel into the prepared tin and sprinkle with the remaining fleur de sel. Leave to set for about 30–40 minutes until firm.

• Once the caramel is firm enough to cut remove from the tin and cut into 2 × 3 cm (¾ × 1¼ in) pieces on a chopping board. Wrap in greaseproof (wax) paper and store in an airtight container in a cool dry place for up to a week.

Fleur de Sel

& Fondant Rings

preparation time : 20 minutes
cook time : 40–45 minutes, plus setting

TOOLS:

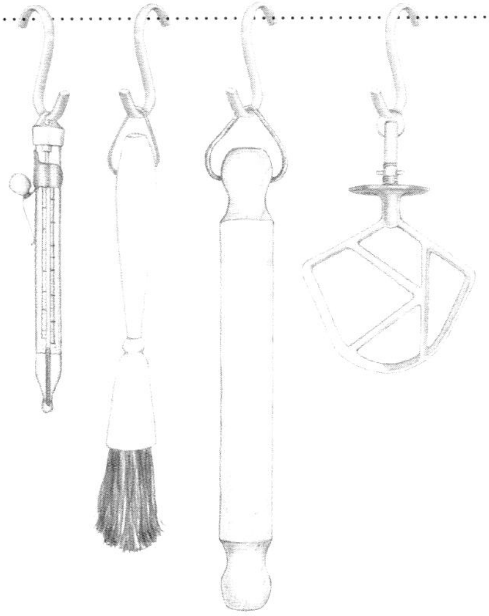

1 batch of Fleur de sel caramels mixture (page 48)
Icing (confectioners') sugar for dusting
250 g (9 oz) cooked fondant (see page 54)

makes 20 *pieces*

- Line a 30 × 21 cm (12 × 8¼ in) rectangular baking tray with baking paper.
- Once the fleur de sel caramel has been made, pour the mixture onto the prepared baking tray and leave to set for 10–15 minutes, making sure that it is still pliable when rolling.
- Lightly dust the work surface with icing sugar and roll the fondant out into a rectangle, a similar size to the caramel, then roll out to a thickness of about 5 mm (¼ in).
- Remove the set caramel and place onto a piece of baking paper. Place the piece of rolled-out fondant onto the caramel and press gently to sandwich.

Roll up the caramel fondant in baking paper as if making a Swiss (jelly) roll. Ensure that it is tightly rolled. The caramel fondant should still be pliable and easy to roll. If the caramel is hardening, use a heat lamp or put the caramel fondant in a warm oven for a few minutes to soften.

- Leave to stand for about 20 minutes until firm, then unwrap the baking paper and, using a serrated knife, slice the caramel fondant into 1–2 cm (½–¾ in) thick slices on a chopping board.
- Wrap each caramel fondant in greaseproof (wax) paper and store in an airtight container in a cool dry place for up to 2 weeks.

4

Fondants & Licorice

Cream Fondant

(cooked method)

1 Place 200 g (7 oz) granulated sugar, 60 ml (2 fl oz/¼ cup) water and 15 ml (½ fl oz) liquid glucose in a heavy-based saucepan.

2 Place the pan over a medium heat and stir until the sugar has dissolved.

3 Insert a sugar thermometer and bring the mixture to the boil, then reduce the heat and simmer until the mixture reaches 121°C (250°F).

4 Transfer the mixture to a freestanding food mixer with a paddle attachment. Add 25 g (1 oz) butter and 1 teaspoon vanilla extract, then beat on a medium speed until the mixture thickens and turns opaque.

5 Add 4 g (¼ oz) cornflour (cornstarch) and continue to beat for another minute.

6 Remove the mixture and place it on a lightly dusted work surface. Knead the fondant for 5 minutes, or until it is smooth, adding more cornflour if neccessary to prevent it from sticking to the work surface. Wrap the fondant in plastic wrap and use it to make Fleur de sel & fondant rings (page 50). The fondant can be stored in an airtight container for up to 2 weeks.

1

2

3

4

5

6

Cream Fondants

(cold method)

preparation time : 20 minutes, plus drying
cook time : none

250 g (9 oz/2 cups) icing (confectioners') sugar, plus extra for dusting

2 tablespoons thick (heavy/double) cream

60 g (2 oz) unsalted butter, softened

2 drops of food colouring of your choice

TOOLS:

makes
350 g
(12½ oz)

• Line a baking tray with baking paper and lightly dust a silicone candy mould with icing sugar.

• Place the icing sugar, cream and softened butter in a food mixer with a paddle attachment. Beat on low speed until all the ingredients are well combined and the mixture forms a soft dough.

• Remove the dough from the bowl and divide into batches, then colour and flavour each with food colouring and flavouring. Knead each dough on a work surface lightly dusted with icing sugar until well combined and smooth.

• Take small balls of the mixture and gently press into the candy mould ensuring to fill each mould completely to the top. Alternatively, you can roll out to 1 cm (½ in) thickness and cut out using a shaped cutter.

• Slowly release the fondants out of the moulds and place onto the prepared baking tray to dry. Leave to dry for at least 5 hours, or preferably overnight. Store in an airtight container in a cool dry place for up to 2 weeks.

Peppermint Creams

preparation time : 15 minutes, plus drying
cook time : none

TOOLS:

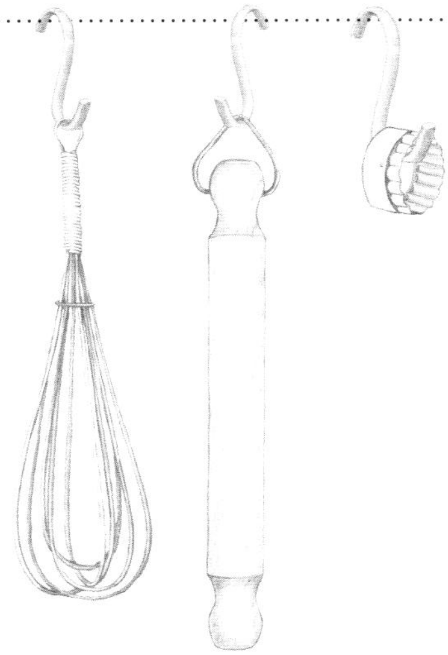

1 egg white

350 g (12½ oz) icing (confectioners') sugar, sifted, plus extra for dusting

½ teaspoon peppermint extract

Food colouring (optional)

makes
380 g
(13½ oz)

- Line a baking tray with baking paper.
- Beat the egg white in a large bowl until foamy then add the sifted icing sugar and peppermint extract and colouring, if using. Mix well until combined.
- Lightly dust the work surface with some icing sugar and knead the mixture for 5 minutes. Roll out the mixture into a 1 cm (½ in) thickness and cut into 4 cm (1½ in) rounds with a fluted pastry cutter.
- Place the rounds on the prepared baking tray and leave to dry for at least 3 hours, or preferably overnight. Store in an airtight container in a cool dry place for up to 2 weeks.

Coffee Liquor

Fondant-Filled Chocolates

preparation time : 20 minutes
cook time : 15 minutes, plus cooling and setting

TOOLS:

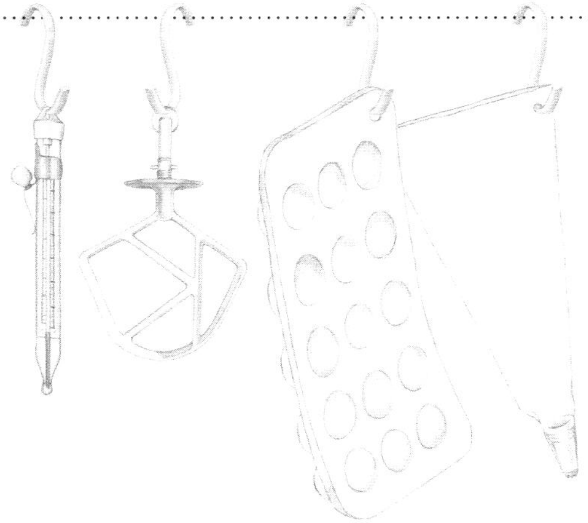

200 g (7 oz) granulated sugar
60 ml (2 fl oz/¼ cup) water
15 ml (½ fl oz) liquid glucose
25 g (1 oz) unsalted butter
1 teaspoon coffee extract
1 teaspoon Irish cream flavouring
500 g (1 lb 2 oz) dark chocolate (at least 70% cocoa solids), tempered (see pages 126–9)

makes
35–40
pieces

• Heat the sugar, water and liquid glucose in a heavy-based saucepan over a medium heat and stir until the sugar has dissolved.

• Insert a sugar thermometer and bring the mixture to the boil. Reduce the heat and simmer until it reaches 121°C (250°F).

• Remove the pan from the heat and add the butter, coffee extract and Irish cream flavouring. Stir well. Transfer the mixture to a freestanding food mixer with a paddle attachment and beat on a medium speed until the mixture thickens slightly and turns opaque.

• Meanwhile, fill the chocolate moulds with the tempered dark chocolate (see pages 126–9) and leave it to set.

• Once the fondant mixture has cooled and slightly thickened but still runny, place it into a piping bag and pipe into the chocolate moulds almost to the top. Leave to set for about 15 minutes then cover the fondants with more chocolate as described on page 130. Leave to set for at least 3–4 hours before unmoulding. Store the fondant chocolates in an airtight container at room temperature for up to 3 weeks.

Firm Ball Stage

118–121°C

(244–250°F)

1 Place the sugar and water in a heavy-based saucepan.

2 Heat for 5–10 minutes until the sugar has dissolved.

3 Insert a sugar thermometer into the saucepan and boil the mixture.

4 If the sugar is crystallising around the saucepan, clean around the sides of the saucepan with a damp pastry brush to prevent this.

5 Once the sugar syrup reaches the correct temperature, it has reached the firm ball stage.

6 To check it has reached this stage, drop a little of the sugar syrup into a bowl of cold water – the sugar will turn into a firm ball that is pliable and keeps its shape when removed from the water.

1

2

3

4

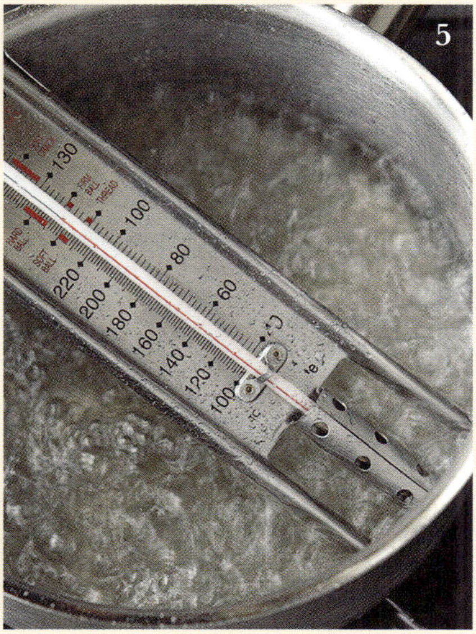
5

6

Licorice

preparation time : 20 minutes
cook time : 1 hour, plus cooling and setting

TOOLS:

- Vegetable oil for oiling
- 200 ml (7 fl oz) water
- 4 tablespoons powdered gelatine
- 40 g (1½ oz/⅓ cup) cornflour (cornstarch)
- 250 g (9 oz) granulated sugar
- 150 ml (5 fl oz) golden syrup (corn syrup)
- 150 ml (5 fl oz) condensed milk
- 85 ml (2¾ fl oz) black treacle (molasses)
- 120 g (4½ oz) unsalted butter
- Pinch of salt
- 3–4 tablespoons black colouring
- 2 teaspoons licorice oil flavouring

makes
60
wheels

• Lightly oil 2 large baking trays and set aside.

• Place the water in a small bowl and sprinkle over the gelatine powder. Leave to soak for 5 minutes, then add the cornflour and mix well.

• Combine the sugar, golden syrup, condensed milk, black treacle, butter and salt in a saucepan. Place over the heat and stir until the sugar has dissolved. Stir in the gelatine mixture and mix well.

• Bring to the boil and insert a sugar thermometer. Cook the mixture until it reaches 121°C (250°F). While the mixture is cooking, add enough black colouring to achieve the right colour.

• Remove from the heat, add the licorice oil flavouring and mix well, then pour onto the prepared baking trays and leave for about 30 minutes until set and firm.

• Unmould the licorice and cut into long strips about 5 mm (¼ in) in width on a chopping board. Roll them into spiral wheels then place them on baking paper and leave to cool completely for 1 hour. Store in an airtight container in a cool dry place for up to a week.

Licorice Allsorts

with Fondant

preparation time : 20 minutes, plus drying
cook time : none

TOOLS:

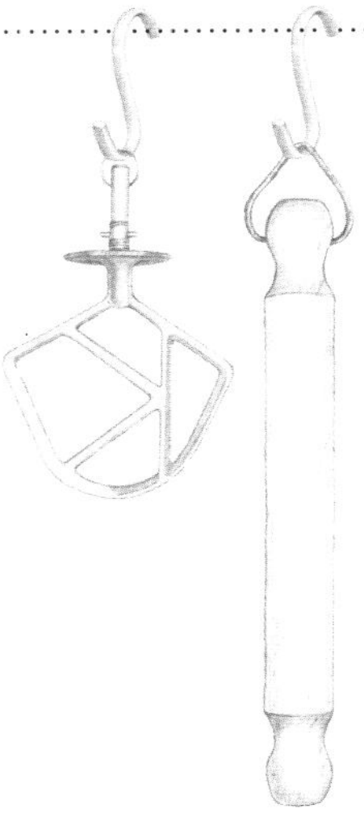

250 g (9 oz/2 cups) icing (confectioners') sugar, plus extra for dusting

2 tablespoons thick (double/heavy) cream

60 g (2 oz) unsalted butter, softened

Tiny amount of food colouring paste (black and any other colours of choice)

1 teaspoon licorice oil flavouring

4 tablespoons sugar sprinkles

makes
350 g
(12½ oz)

• Line a baking tray with baking paper.

• Place the icing sugar, cream and softened butter in a food mixer with a paddle attachment. Beat on low speed until all the ingredients are well combined and form a soft dough.

• Remove the dough from the bowl and divide into batches. Colour with the different colours, leaving some white. Flavour the black coloured fondant with the licorice oil flavouring.

• Lightly dust the work surface with icing sugar and knead each dough for 5 minutes until well combined and smooth.

• Roll out to 5 mm (¼ in) thickness, sandwich the different colours together and cut out 2 cm (¾ in) squares with a sharp knife. Make different shapes like discs then roll all the pieces in sugar sprinkles. Place the shapes onto the prepared baking tray and leave to dry for at least 5 hours, or preferably overnight. Store in an airtight container in a cool dry place for up to a week.

Licorice Laces

preparation time : 20 minutes
cook time : 1 hour, plus setting and drying

TOOLS:

Vegetable oil for oiling
200 ml (7 fl oz) water
4 tablespoons powdered gelatine
40 g (1½ oz/⅓ cup) cornflour (cornstarch)
250 g (9 oz) granulated sugar
150 ml (5 fl oz) golden syrup (corn syrup)
200 ml (7 fl oz) condensed milk
100 g (3½ oz) unsalted butter
Pinch of salt
½–1 teaspoon red food colouring paste
1 teaspoon licorice oil flavouring
1 teaspoon strawberry oil flavouring
Icing (confectioners') sugar for dusting

makes
650 g
(1 lb 7 oz)

• Lightly oil 2 large baking trays and set aside. Place the water in a small bowl and sprinkle over the gelatine. Leave to soak for 5 minutes, then add the cornflour and mix well.

• Combine the granulated sugar, golden syrup, condensed milk, butter and salt in a saucepan. Place over the heat and stir until the sugar has dissolved. Stir in the gelatine mixture and mix well.

• Bring to the boil and insert a sugar thermometer. Cook the mixture until it reaches 121°C (250°F). While the mixture is cooking, add the red colouring and mix well.

• Remove from the heat, add the licorice and strawberry oil flavourings and mix well. Pour the mixture onto the prepared baking trays and leave for about 30–45 minutes until set and firm.

• Unmould the licorice onto a chopping board lightly dusted with icing sugar and, using a sharp knife, cut into 3 mm (⅛ in) width strips to form laces. Place them on baking paper and leave to cool and dry completely for about 1 hour. Store in an airtight container in a cool dry place for up to a week.

How to Pull Sugar

1 After making the sugar syrup (see page 72), carefully pour it onto an oiled marble slab or silicone mat.

2 As the syrup is runny at this stage, work quickly, using a palette knife or metal scraper, and gently push or scrape the outer edges of the sugar inwards to the middle. Keep working the syrup by doing this until the syrup starts to cool down and thicken.

3 Add flavouring or colouring if desired and continue to push the syrup back and forth to ensure it is mixed in well.

4 Once the syrup is cool enough to handle, put on some latex gloves and lightly oil them. Start pulling the now thickened syrup, bringing the ends together.

5 Pull and bring the ends back together as this aerates the syrup and makes it chewy. Repeat this until it is difficult to pull any more.

6 The taffy is now changed to a lighter shade in colour and is still pliable.

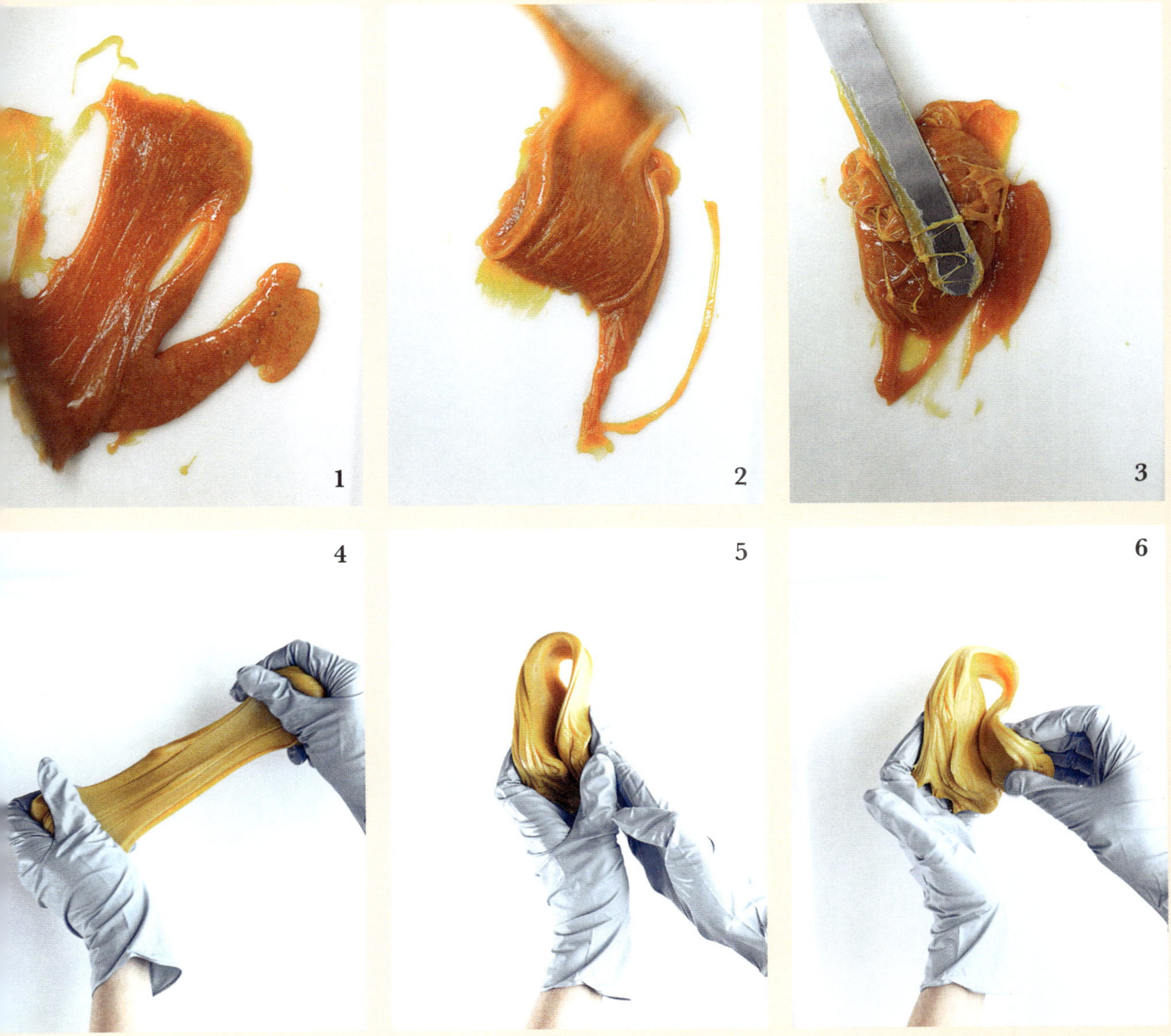
1
2
3
4
5
6

Taffy

Chewy Fruit Candies

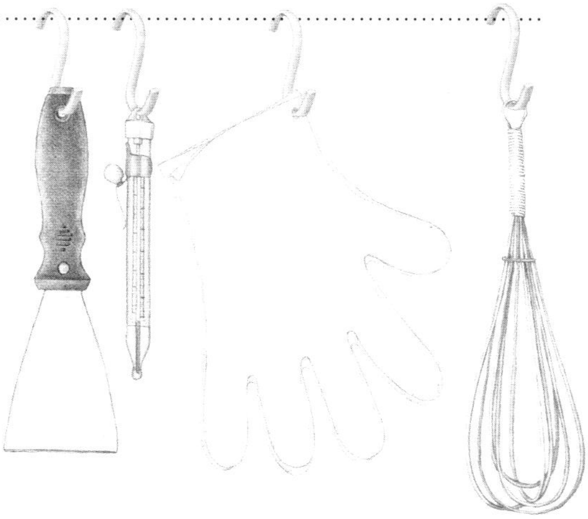

preparation time : 25 minutes
cook time : 20–30 minutes

TOOLS:

Vegetable oil for oiling
200 g (7 oz) granulated sugar
125 ml (4 fl oz/½ cup) golden syrup (corn syrup)
2 teaspoons cornflour (cornstarch)
60 ml (2 fl oz/¼ cup) water
15 g (½ oz) unsalted butter
¼ teaspoon bicarbonate of soda (baking soda)
2 drops of strawberry flavouring
Tiny amount of pink colouring paste
1 teaspoon citric acid (optional)

makes 40 *pieces*

• Lightly oil a marble slab or a silicone mat and a metal scraper or palette knives.

• Heat the sugar, syrup, cornflour, water and butter in a saucepan over a low heat and whisk until smooth then, using a wooden spoon, stir until the sugar has dissolved. Increase the heat, insert a sugar thermometer and cook until the mixture reaches 121°C (250°F).

• Remove from the heat and add the bicarbonate of soda, stirring until combined. Carefully pour the syrup onto the oiled marble slab or silicone mat. As the syrup is runny at this stage, work quickly, using the metal scraper to gently push or scrape the outer edges of the sugar inwards to the middle. Keep doing this until the syrup starts to cool down and thicken.

• Add the flavouring, colouring and citric acid, if using, and push the syrup inwards, making sure it is mixed in.

• Once the syrup is cool enough to handle, wearing a pair of lightly oiled latex gloves, start pulling the thickened syrup, bringing the ends together. Repeat doing this until it is difficult to pull the taffy. The taffy is now a lighter shade of colour and still pliable.

• Divide the mixture and place on a lightly oiled marble slab. Roll the taffy into a rope until it is 5 mm (¼ in) thick in diameter. Using the metal scraper, cut the taffy into 2.5 cm (1 in) lengths, then wrap in greaseproof (wax) paper or cellophane. Store in an airtight container in a cool dry place for up to a week.

5

Pâte de Fruit & Jelly Sweets

Raspberry
Pâte de Fruit

preparation time : 10 minutes
cook time : 45–60 minutes, plus cooling and drying

580 g (1 lb 4 oz) granulated sugar
10 g (¼ oz) pectin powder
500 ml (17 fl oz/2 cups) raspberry purée
Juice of 1 lemon
100 g (3½ oz) caster (superfine) sugar for rolling

TOOLS:

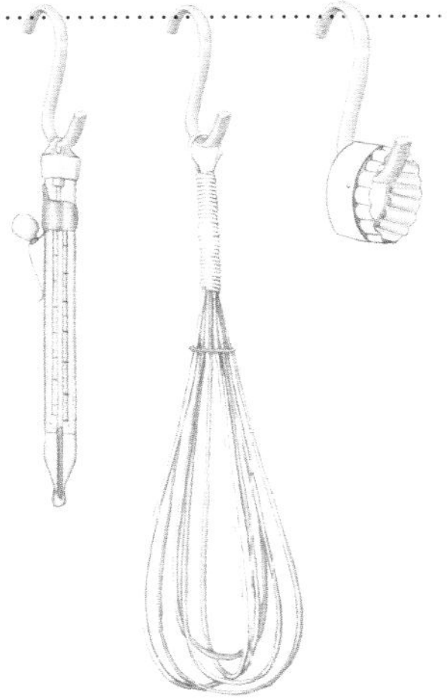

makes
36
squares

- Line a 19 cm (7½ in) square baking tin with plastic wrap.
- Place half the granulated sugar and the pectin powder in a small bowl and mix thoroughly.
- Combine the raspberry purée, the remaining granulated sugar and the lemon juice in a heavy-based saucepan and put onto the heat. Stir until the sugar has dissolved, then whisk in the sugar and pectin mix.
- Insert a sugar thermometer and bring the mixture to the boil. Reduce the heat and keep the mixture on a constant simmer until it reaches 118°C (244°F). Keep stirring the mixture to make sure it doesn't catch and burn on the base of the pan.
- Once the pâte de fruit mixture has reached the correct temperature, remove the pan from the heat and leave to cool slightly.
- Pour the fruit mixture into the prepared baking tin and leave to cool completely at room temperature. Cover with more plastic wrap and then leave to set, preferably overnight.
- Once firm, unmould the pâte de fruit and cut into squares or cut out using shaped cutters as desired. Place the caster sugar in a shallow dish or tray and roll the pâte de fruit shapes in the sugar, then place on a baking paper-lined tray and leave to dry out overnight in a cool dry place.
- Store in a loosely covered container at room temperature in a dry place for up to 2 weeks.

Blackberry & Licorice

Pâte de Fruit

preparation time : 10 minutes
cook time : 45–60 minutes, plus cooling, setting and drying

TOOLS:

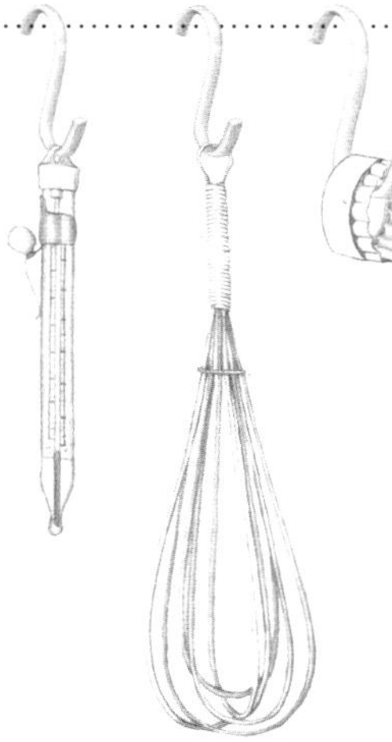

580 g (1 lb 4 oz) granulated sugar
10 g (¼ oz) pectin powder
500 ml (17 fl oz/2 cups) blackberry purée
Juice of ½ lemon
1 teaspoon licorice flavouring oil
100 g (3½ oz) caster (superfine) sugar for rolling

makes
100
rounds

• Line a 21 cm (8¼ in) square baking tin with plastic wrap.

• Place half the granulated sugar and the pectin powder in a small bowl and mix thoroughly.

• Combine the blackberry purée, the remaining granulated sugar and the lemon juice in a heavy-based saucepan and put onto the heat. Stir until the sugar has dissolved, then whisk in the sugar and pectin mix.

• Insert a sugar thermometer and bring the mixture to the boil. Reduce the heat and keep the mixture on a constant simmer until it reaches 118°C (244°F). Keep stirring the mixture to make sure it doesn't catch and burn on the base of the pan.

• Once the pâte de fruit mixture has reached the correct temperature, remove from the heat, add the licorice flavouring and leave to cool slightly.

• Pour the fruit mixture into the prepared baking tin and leave to cool completely. Cover with more plastic wrap and leave to set, preferably overnight.

• Once firm, unmould the pâte de fruit and, using a 2 cm (¾ in) round cutter, cut into rounds or cut out using shaped cutters as desired. Place the caster sugar in a shallow dish or tray and roll the pâte de fruit shapes in the sugar, then place on a baking paper-lined tray and leave to dry out overnight in a cool dry place. Store in a loosely covered container at room temperature in a dry place for up to 2 weeks.

Quince
Pâte de Fruit

preparation time : 15 minutes
cook time : 2½ hours, plus cooling and setting

TOOLS:

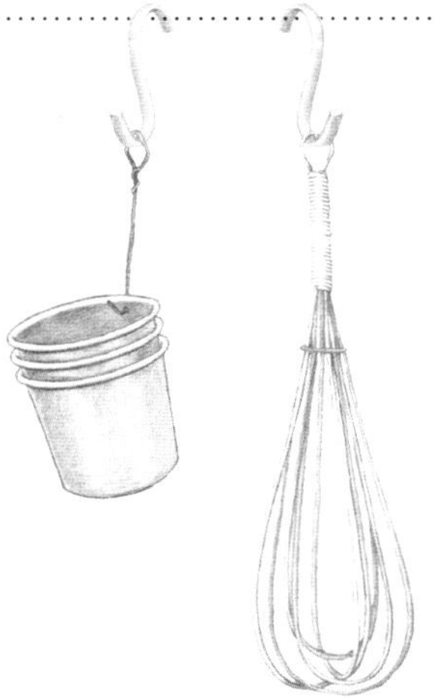

Vegetable oil for oiling
1 kg (2 lb 3 oz) quince, peeled, cored and cut into chunks
Juice of 1 lemon
580 g (1 lb 4 oz) granulated sugar
10 g (¼ oz) pectin powder
100 g (3½ oz) caster (superfine) sugar for dusting

makes 6 *pieces*

• Lightly oil six 125 ml (4 fl oz/½ cup) dariole moulds.

• Place the quince in a pan, cover with water and add the lemon juice. Bring to the boil, then reduce the heat and simmer for 20–30 minutes until the quince is soft and tender. Drain the quince and blitz in a food processor to a purée. The mixture should measure 500 ml (17 fl oz/2 cups).

• Place half the granulated sugar and the pectin powder in a small bowl and mix thoroughly.

• Combine the quince purée and the remaining granulated sugar in a heavy-based saucepan and put onto the heat. Stir until the sugar has dissolved, then whisk in the sugar and pectin mix.

• Bring the mixture to the boil. Reduce the heat and keep the mixture constantly simmering, stirring all the time, until the mixture becomes a thick paste and comes away from the sides of the saucepan. This will take about 1¾–2 hours.

• Remove the pan from the heat and leave to cool slightly. Spoon the mixture into the prepared moulds and leave to cool completely. Cover with more plastic wrap and leave to set, preferably overnight.

• Once firm, unmould the pâte de fruit and serve with cheese or cut into small cubes and dust with caster sugar, if desired, to create sweets. Store in an airtight container in the refrigerator for up to 6 months.

Jelly Sweets

preparation time : 15 minutes
cook time : 20–30 minutes, plus cooling and setting

TOOLS:

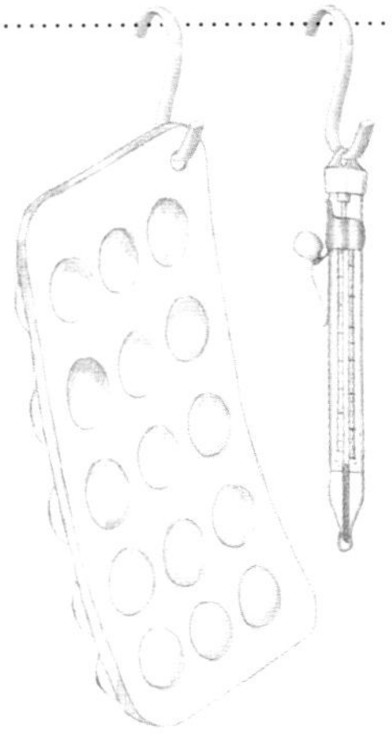

Vegetable oil for oiling
100 g (3½ oz) caster (superfine) sugar
25 ml (¾ fl oz) citric acid
420 ml (14 fl oz) water
4 tablespoons powdered gelatine
5 g (¼ oz) cornflour (cornstarch)
275 g (9½ oz/1¼ cups) granulated sugar
30 ml (1 fl oz) liquid glucose
1 teaspoon strawberry or orange flavouring oil
1 drop each of a selection of food colourings

makes
12–15
shapes

• Lightly oil various shaped sweet moulds.

• Combine the caster sugar and the 3 teaspoons of citric acid in a small bowl and set aside. Place 150 ml (5 fl oz) water in another small bowl and sprinkle over the gelatine. Leave to soak for 5 minutes, then add the cornflour and mix well.

• Heat the granulated sugar, the remaining water and liquid glucose in a heavy-based saucepan over the heat and bring to a gentle boil. Add the gelatine mixture, stirring all the time to avoid any lumps.

• Insert a sugar thermometer and cook until it reaches 118°C (244°F). Once the mixture reaches the correct temperature, remove the pan from the heat and carefully add the remaining citric acid and the flavouring. Stir until thoroughly mixed.

• Divide the mixture and pour into pitchers and add colourings of your choice. Slowly fill the sweet mould with the coloured mixtures and leave to cool and set in a cool place for about 30 minutes.

• Once cooled and set, unmould and dust the sweets in the caster sugar/citric acid mixture. Store in an airtight container for up to 3 weeks.

6

Marshmallow, Nougat & Turkish Delight

Basic Marshmallow

preparation time : 20 minutes
cook time : 20–30 minutes, plus cooling and setting

TOOLS:

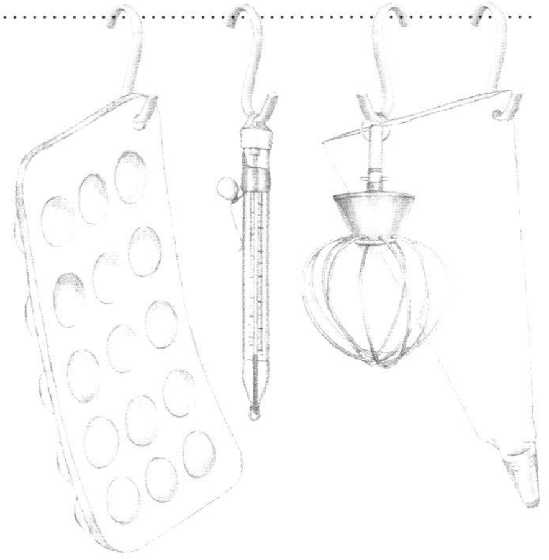

Vegetable oil for oiling
250 ml (8½ fl oz/1 cup) water
30 g (1 oz) powdered gelatine
300 g (10½ oz) granulated sugar
100 ml (3½ fl oz) liquid glucose
2 egg whites
Pinch of salt
1 teaspoon vanilla extract
400 g (14 oz) caster (superfine) sugar
2 drops of food colouring (blue, green, pink)

makes 24 *pieces*

• Lightly oil two 12-hole deep candy moulds.

• Place 100 ml (3½ fl oz) water in a small bowl, sprinkle over the gelatine and leave to soak for 5 minutes.

• Heat the granulated sugar, 150 ml (5 fl oz) water and the liquid glucose in a saucepan, stirring until the sugar has dissolved. Bring the mixture to the boil, insert a sugar thermometer and cook until it reaches 121°C (250°F). Remove from the heat, add the soaked gelatine and stir until combined and melted.

• Whisk the egg whites and salt in a freestanding mixer on a medium speed until the mixture forms soft peaks. Add the vanilla extract and, while whisking, slowly add the hot sugar gelatine mixture in a thin steady stream. Whisk until all the mixture is used up and the meringue is cool and thickened.

• Divide the caster sugar into different bowls, add the colourings and mix until the sugar is evenly coloured.

• Place the cooled meringue mixture into a piping bag with a plain nozzle and pipe into the prepared moulds. Tap the moulds to ensure no air bubbles are trapped, sprinkle some coloured sugar over the tops and leave to set for at least 2 hours.

• Slowly remove the marshmallows from the moulds and gently roll into more coloured sugar. Place the marshmallows on baking paper to dry. Store in an airtight container for up to 2 weeks.

Caramel Marshmallow
Filled Chocolates

preparation time : 1 hour–1 hour 40 minutes
cook time : 20–30 minutes, plus 30–40 minutes setting

TOOLS:

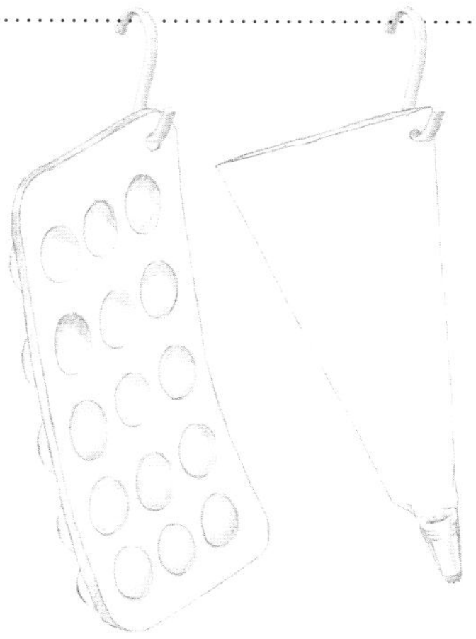

500 g (1 lb 2 oz) dark chocolate (at least 70% cocoa solids), tempered (see pages 126–9)
250 g (9 oz) Basic soft caramel (page 168)
1 batch of Basic marshmallow (page 86)
3 tablespoons raw (demerara) sugar for sprinkling

makes
45
cups

• Cover chocolate cup moulds with the tempered chocolate, following the instructions for covering chocolate cup shells on page 130.

• Fill a piping bag with the soft caramel and fill the chocolate cup shells quarter full.

• Once the marshmallow has been made, fill a piping bag with a star nozzle with the mixture and pipe the marshmallow over the caramels setting in the chocolate cup shells. Sprinkle the marshmallow tops with raw sugar and leave to set for at least 2 hours. Store in an airtight container in a cool dry place for up to a week.

Strawberries & Cream

Marshmallow Twists

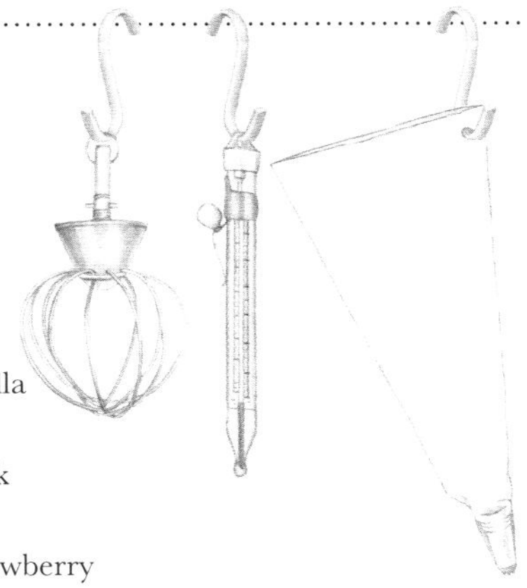

preparation time : 15 minutes
cook time : 20–30 minutes, plus cooling and setting

TOOLS:

50 g (1¾ oz) icing (confectioners') sugar
50 g (1¾ oz) cornflour (cornstarch)
200 ml (7 fl oz) water
30 g (1 oz) powdered gelatine
300 g (10½ oz) granulated sugar
50 ml (1¾ fl oz) evaporated milk
75 ml (2½ fl oz) liquid glucose
2 egg whites
Pinch of salt
1 teaspoon vanilla extract
¼ teaspoon pink colouring
½ teaspoon strawberry flavouring

makes
6
long twists

- Line a baking tray with baking paper. Combine the icing sugar and cornflour in a small bowl and sprinkle over the prepared baking tray.
- Place 100 ml (3½ fl oz) of the water in a small bowl, sprinkle over the gelatine and leave to soak for 5 minutes.
- Heat the sugar, the remaining water, the evaporated milk and liquid glucose together in a saucepan and stir until the sugar has dissolved. Bring the mixture to the boil, then insert a sugar thermometer and cook the mixture until it reaches 121°C (250°F).
- Remove from the heat, add the soaked gelatine and stir well until combined and melted.
- Whisk the egg whites and salt in a freestanding food mixer on a medium speed until it forms soft peaks. Add the vanilla extract and, while whisking, slowly add the hot sugar gelatine mixture in a thin steady stream. Whisk until all the mixture is used up and the meringue is cooled and thickened.
- Divide the mixture into 2 bowls. In one, stir in the pink colouring and strawberry flavouring.
- Place both mixtures into a duo piping bag with a star nozzle and pipe little twists onto the icing sugar/cornflour lined baking tray. Leave to set for at least 2 hours at room temperature. Store in an airtight container for up to 2 weeks.

Corn & Marshmallow

Caramel Clusters

preparation time : 15 minutes
cook time : 20 minutes, plus cooling and setting

TOOLS:

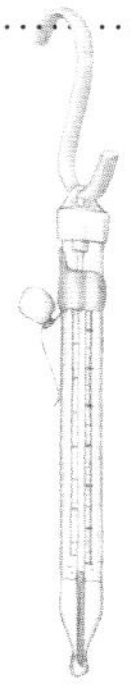

100 g (3½ oz) Strawberries & cream marshmallow twists (page 90)
100 g (3½ oz) salted popcorn
30 g (1 oz/1 cup) cornflakes
50 g (1¾ oz) dried cranberries
250 g (9 oz) soft brown sugar
125 ml (4 fl oz/½ cup) thick (double/heavy) cream
1 tablespoon golden syrup (corn syrup)
30 g (1 oz) unsalted butter

makes 12–15 *pieces*

- Line a baking tray with baking paper.
- Cut the marshmallows into small pieces, then place in a large bowl with the popcorn, cornflakes and dried cranberries. Set aside.
- Heat the sugar, cream, golden syrup and butter in a saucepan, stirring until the sugar has dissolved. Bring the mixture to the boil, then insert a sugar thermometer and cook until the mixture reaches 125°C (257°F).
- Once the sugar mixture reaches the correct temperature, remove the pan from the heat and leave to cool for 5 minutes.
- Stir the caramel mixture into the bowl of popcorn, marshmallow, cornflakes and cranberries. Mix well and place tablespoonfuls of the mixture in clusters on the prepared baking tray.
- Leave to set for at least 20 minutes at room temperature. Store in an airtight container for up to a week.

Chocolate-Coated Marshmallows

preparation time : 30–35 minutes
cook time : 15–20 minutes, plus cooling and setting

TOOLS:

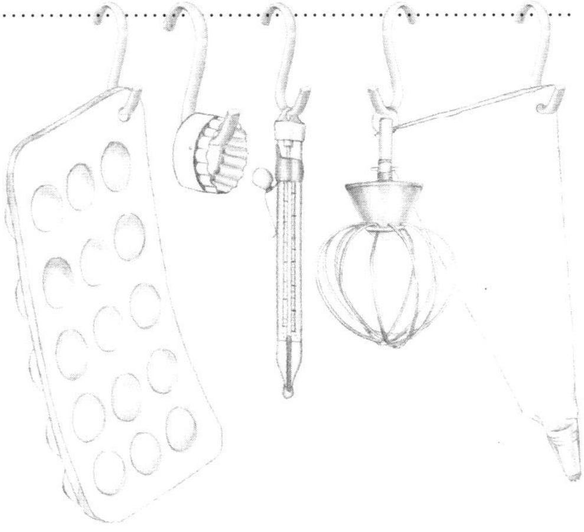

Vegetable oil for oiling
500 g (1 lb 2 oz) milk chocolate
10 caramel wafers
80 ml (2½ fl oz/⅓ cup) water
12 g (½ oz) powdered gelatine
200 g (7 oz) caster (superfine) sugar
1 tablespoon liquid glucose
100 g (3½ oz) egg whites (4 egg whites)
Pinch of salt

makes
10
marshmallows

• Oil 10 cake push pop containers (see above) or cylinders with a diameter of 4.5 cm (1¾ in). Line 2 baking trays with baking paper. Melt 50 g (1¾ oz) of the chocolate (see page 126). Cut out rounds of the wafers with a 4.5 cm (1¾ in) pastry cutter. Dip one side of the wafer rounds into the chocolate and place on the baking trays, chocolate side up. Leave for 2 hours. Turn them so the wafer is facing up.

• Put 2 tablespoons water in a small bowl, sprinkle the gelatine over and leave to soak for 5 minutes.

• Heat the sugar, liquid glucose and the remaining 2 tablespoons water in a pan over a medium heat, stirring until the sugar has dissolved. Bring to the boil, insert a sugar thermometer and cook until the syrup reaches 120°C (248°F), then leave on the heat, add the gelatine and stir for 1 minute until melted.

• Whisk the egg whites and salt in a freestanding mixer on a medium speed until soft peaks start to form. Increase the speed to high and pour in the sugar syrup in a thin stream, whisking until the mixture is used. Whisk for 10–15 minutes until the mixture is cool, thick and holds soft firm peaks. Spoon the mixture into a piping bag with a large plain nozzle and pipe into the containers to three-quarters full. Leave for 4 hours or overnight.

• Melt and temper the remaining chocolate (see pages 126–9). Dip the marshmallow bases into the chocolate, then sit them on top of the wafers. Leave for 10 minutes. Put them on a wire rack with a baking tray underneath and ladle the chocolate over. Let any excess chocolate drip down. Leave for a few minutes before putting them on lined baking trays. Leave for 3–4 hours. Store in a container for a week.

Basic Nougat

Pistachios, Almonds & Cherries

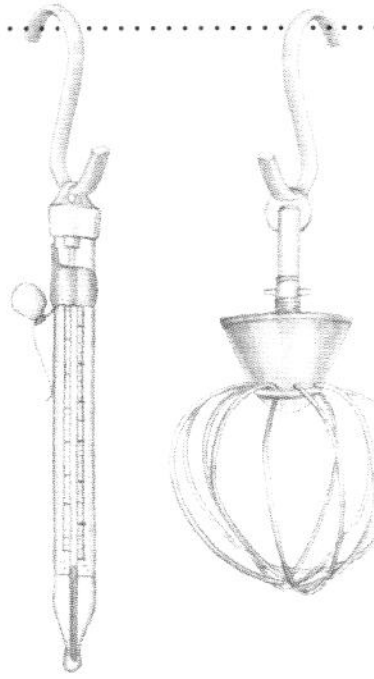

preparation time : 15 minutes
cook time : 20–35 minutes, plus cooling

TOOLS:

Vegetable oil for oiling
4 small sheets or 2 large sheets of rice paper
300 g (10½ oz) granulated sugar
50 ml (1¾ fl oz) water
150 ml (5 fl oz) honey
1 large egg white
100 g (3½ oz/⅔ cup) pistachio nuts, toasted
100 g (3½ oz/⅔ cup) blanched almonds, toasted
50 g (1¾ oz) dried cherries

makes
5
long strips

• Lightly oil and line a 19 cm (7½ in) square tin with baking paper, then with 1 or 2 sheets of rice paper.

• Heat the sugar, water and honey in a heavy-based saucepan over a medium heat and stir until the sugar has dissolved. Bring to the boil, insert a sugar thermometer and cook until the mixture reaches 120°C (248°F) for a very soft nougat, 143°C (289°F) for a soft nougat and 150°C (302°F) for a firm nougat.

• Meanwhile, whisk the egg white in a freestanding food mixer until soft peaks form. Once the syrup has reached the correct temperature, remove from the heat and slowly pour the sugar mixture into the meringue while still whisking on medium speed. Whisk until the mixture thickens and turns creamy in colour. Stir in the nuts and cherries and mix well.

• Spoon the mixture into the prepared tin and level the top. Place another sheet or 2 of rice paper on top, pressing gently. Leave to cool completely for at least 3–4 hours, or preferably overnight at room temperature before cutting into pieces or strips. Store in an airtight container with baking paper between the pieces or strips for up to 2 weeks.

Tiramisu Nougat

preparation time : 15 minutes
cook time : 30–35 minutes, plus setting

TOOLS:

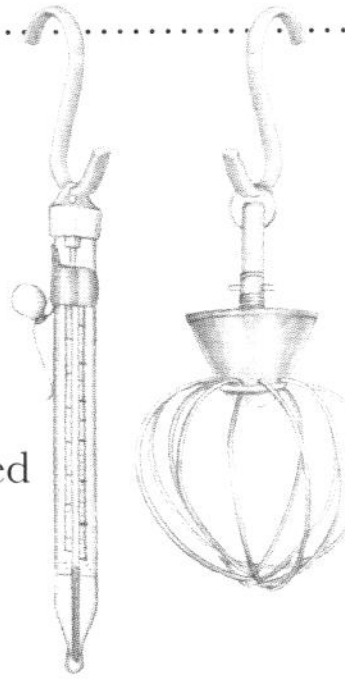

Vegetable oil for oiling
2 small sheets or 1 large sheet of rice paper
20 g (3/4 oz) unsweetened (Dutch) cocoa powder
2 teaspoons instant espresso powder
300 g (10 1/2 oz) granulated sugar
50 ml (1 3/4 fl oz) water
150 ml (5 fl oz) honey
1 large egg white
100 g (3 1/2 oz/2/3 cup) whole blanched almonds, toasted
30 g (1 oz) amaretti cookies

makes 16 *squares*

- Lightly oil and line the base of a 19 cm (7 1/2 in) square tin with rice paper.
- Mix the cocoa powder with 1 teaspoon espresso powder together in a small bowl and set aside.
- Heat the sugar, water and honey in a heavy-based saucepan over a medium heat and stir until the sugar has dissolved. Bring to the boil, insert a sugar thermometer and cook until the mixture reaches 130°C (266°F).
- Meanwhile, whisk the egg white in a freestanding food mixer until soft peaks form.
- Once the syrup has reached the correct temperature, remove from the heat and stir in the remaining espresso powder. Slowly pour the sugar mixture into the meringue while still whisking on a medium speed. Whisk until the mixture thickens and turns creamy in colour. Stir in the almonds and amaretti cookies and mix well. Spoon the mixture into the prepared tin and level the top. Leave to set at room temperature for about 3–4 hours, or preferably overnight.
- Once set, cut the nougat into large squares and dust with the reserved cocoa and coffee mixture. Store in an airtight container for up to 2 weeks.

Strawberries & Vanilla

Nougat

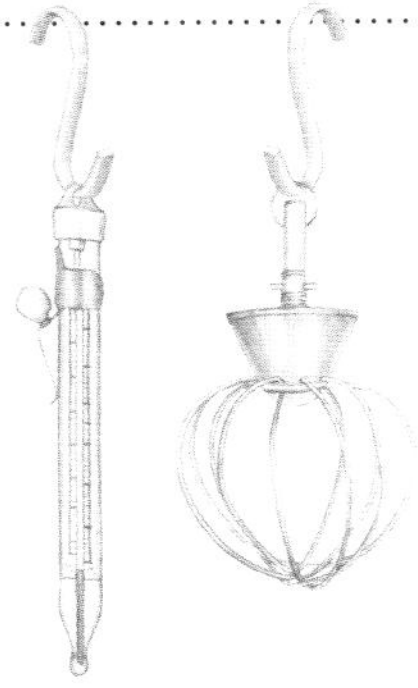

preparation time : 20 minutes
cook time : 1 hour 30–35 minutes, plus cooling and setting

TOOLS:

- 200 g (7 oz/1⅓ cups) fresh strawberries
- Vegetable oil for oiling
- 2 small sheets or 1 large sheet of rice paper
- 300 g (10½ oz) granulated sugar
- 50 ml (1¾ fl oz) water
- 150 ml (5 fl oz) honey
- 1 large egg white
- Seeds from 1 vanilla pod
- 100g (3½ oz/⅔ cup) whole blanched almonds, toasted
- Icing (confectioners') sugar for dusting

makes
5
long strips

• Preheat the oven to 100°C (212°F). Line a baking tray with a silicone baking mat. Slice the strawberries, place them on the prepared baking tray and cook in the oven for 1 hour to dry out.

• Once the strawberries are dried, remove from the oven and leave to cool. Peel away from the silicone mat and set aside.

• Lightly oil and line the base of a 19 cm (7½ in) square tin with rice paper.

• Heat the granulated sugar, water and honey in a heavy-based saucepan over a medium heat and stir until the sugar has dissolved. Bring to the boil, insert a sugar thermometer and cook until the mixture reaches 130°C (266°F).

• Meanwhile, whisk the egg white in a freestanding food mixer until soft peaks form.

• Once the syrup has reached the correct temperature, remove from the heat and stir in the vanilla. Slowly pour the sugar mix into the meringue while still whisking on medium speed. Whisk until the mixture thickens and turns creamy in colour. Stir in half the strawberries and all the almonds.

• Spoon the mixture into the prepared tin and level the top. Place more dried strawberries over the top, pressing gently onto the nougat. Lightly dust with icing sugar and leave at room temperature for 3–4 hours, or preferably overnight before cutting into pieces or strips. Store in an airtight container for up to 2 weeks.

Panforte

preparation time : 15 minutes
cook time : 45–50 minutes, plus cooling

TOOLS:

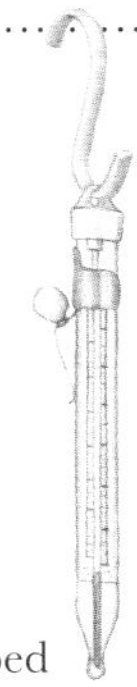

- Vegetable oil for oiling
- 20 g (¾ oz) unsweetened (Dutch) cocoa powder, plus extra for dusting
- 100 g (3½ oz) granulated sugar
- 100 g (3½ oz) honey
- 50 g (1¾ oz) hazelnuts, toasted
- 50 g (1¾ oz/⅓ cup) whole blanched almonds, toasted
- 50 g (1¾ oz) walnut pieces, toasted
- 20 g (¾ oz) dried cherries
- 40 g (1½ oz) dried figs, cut into quarters
- 40 g (1½ oz) candied orange peel, chopped (see page 232)
- 50 g (1¾ oz/⅓ cup) plain (all-purpose) flour
- 50 g (1¾ oz) dark chocolate (at least 70% cocoa solids), finely chopped
- 1 teaspoon ground ginger
- 2 teaspoons ground cinnamon
- ½ teaspoon mixed (pumpkin pie) spice
- 30 g (1 oz) unsalted butter
- Icing (confectioners') sugar for dusting

makes
12
wedges

• Preheat the oven to 160°C (320°F).

• Line the sides and base of a 20 cm (8 in) round loose-based or springform tin with baking paper, then lightly oil the base and dust with cocoa powder.

• Heat the sugar and honey together in a saucepan until the sugar has dissolved. Insert a sugar thermometer and cook until the syrup reaches 115°C (239°F).

• In a large bowl, mix all the dry ingredients, including the remaining cocoa powder and spices together and combine well.

• Once the sugar and honey mixture has reached the correct temperature, remove from the heat and add the butter, then mix well. Pour the mixture over the dry ingredients, stirring to mix well. Pour the mixture into the prepared tin and bake in the oven for 30–35 minutes.

• Remove from the oven and leave to cool in the tin for 10–15 minutes on a wire rack.

• Using a knife, slowly loosen the edges of the panforte around the tin. Remove the base from the side of the tin and leave to cool completely.

• Remove the baking paper from the bottom of the panforte, then dust icing sugar over the top and cut into wedges. Store in an airtight container for up to a week.

Marcona Almond

Turron

preparation time : 10 minutes
cook time : 25–30 minutes, plus cooling

TOOLS:

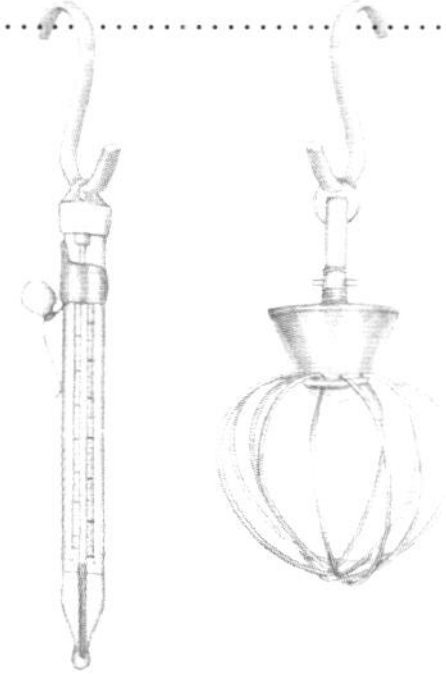

Vegetable oil for oiling
2 large sheets or 4 small sheets of rice paper
300 g (10½ oz) granulated sugar
30 ml (1 fl oz) water
150 ml (5 fl oz) orange blossom honey
1 large egg white
250 g (9 oz) Marcona almonds, toasted
1 teaspoon finely grated lemon zest

makes
5
long strips

• Lightly oil and line the base of a 19 cm (7½ in) square tin with 1 or 2 sheets of rice paper.

• Heat the sugar, water and honey in a heavy-based saucepan over a medium heat and stir until the sugar has dissolved. Bring to the boil, insert a sugar thermometer and boil until the mixture reaches 149°C (300°F).

• Meanwhile, whisk the egg white in a freestanding food mixer until soft peaks form. Once the syrup has reached the correct temperature, remove from the heat and leave to settle. Slowly pour the sugar mixture into the meringue while still whisking on a medium speed. Whisk until the mixture thickens and turns creamy in colour. Stir in the toasted almonds and finely grated lemon zest and mix well.

• Spoon the mixture into the prepared tin and level the top. Place another 1 or 2 sheets of rice paper on top, pressing gently. Leave to cool completely at room temperature for about 3–4 hours before cutting into pieces or strips. Store in an airtight container for up to 3–4 weeks.

Basic Lemon
Turkish Delight

preparation time : 10 minutes
cook time : 50–55 minutes, plus cooling and drying

TOOLS:

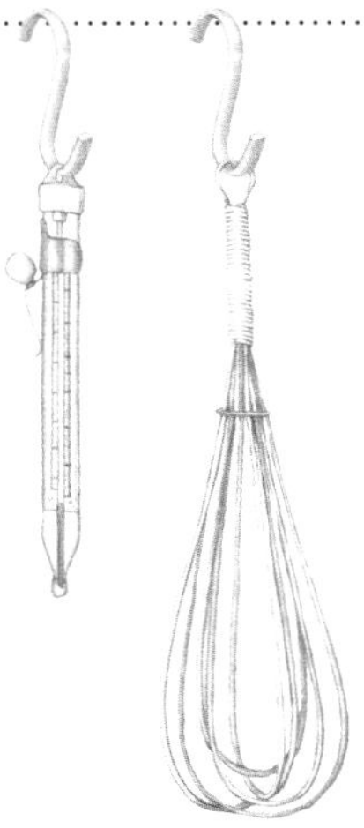

50 g (1¾ oz) icing (confectioners') sugar
85 g (3 oz) cornflour (cornstarch)
470 ml (16 fl oz) water
400 g (14 oz) granulated sugar
2 teaspoons each of lemon juice and finely grated lemon zest
½ teaspoon cream of tartar
1 teaspoon orange blossom water
1 drop of yellow food colouring

makes 30 *pieces*

• Line an 18 cm (7 in) square tin with plastic wrap. Mix the icing sugar and 25 g (1 oz) of the cornflour together in a small bowl and set aside.

• Heat 200 ml (7 fl oz) water, the granulated sugar, lemon juice and zest in a pan, stirring until the sugar has dissolved. Insert a sugar thermometer and cook until the syrup reaches 120°C (248°F).

• Meanwhile, pour the remaining water into another saucepan, add the remaining cornflour and the cream of tartar and stir together ensuring that there are no lumps. Place over a medium heat and bring to the boil, stirring until thick and smooth.

• Once the syrup has reached the correct temperature, remove from the heat and slowly add the syrup a little at a time into the cornflour mixture, whisking constantly until combined. Return the mixture to a low heat and gently simmer for about 30–35 minutes, stirring all the time. The mixture will turn a very light amber colour and thicken. Stir in the orange blossom water and food colouring and simmer for a further 5 minutes.

• Spoon the mixture into the prepared tin and level the top. Cover with more plastic wrap and cool at room temperature for 6–8 hours, or preferably overnight.

• Once cold, peel off the plastic wrap and dust with some of the icing sugar mix. Turn over onto baking paper, peel off the plastic wrap and dust with more icing sugar mixture. Cut into small squares and roll in more icing sugar mixture. Leave to dry overnight. Store in a container for up to 2 weeks.

Rose Petal & Pistachio

Turkish Delight

preparation time : 10 minutes
cook time : 50–55 minutes, plus cooling and drying

TOOLS:

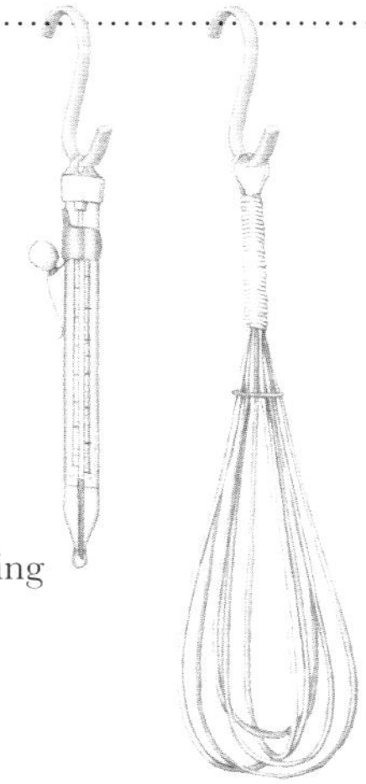

50 g (1¾ oz) icing (confectioners') sugar
85 g (3 oz) cornflour (cornstarch)
470 ml (16 fl oz) water
400 g (14 oz) granulated sugar
1 teaspoon lemon juice
½ teaspoon cream of tartar
2 tablespoons dried rose petals
30 g (1 oz) pistachio nuts, roughly chopped
1 teaspoon rose water
2 drops of pink food colouring

makes
30
pieces

• Line an 18 cm (7 in) square tin with plastic wrap. Combine the icing sugar and 25 g (1 oz) of the cornflour together in a small bowl and set aside.

• Heat 200 ml (7 fl oz) water, granulated sugar and lemon juice in a pan, stirring until the sugar has dissolved. Insert a sugar thermometer and cook until the syrup reaches 120°C (248°F).

• Meanwhile, pour the remaining water into another pan, add the remaining cornflour and the cream of tartar and stir ensuring that there are no lumps. Bring to the boil, stirring until it thickens and is smooth.

• Once the syrup has reached the correct temperature, remove from the heat and slowly add the syrup, a little at a time, whisking until combined. Return to the heat and gently simmer for about 30–35 minutes, stirring all the time. The mixture will turn a very light amber colour and thicken. Stir in the petals, pistachio nuts, rose water and food colouring and simmer for 5 minutes.

• Spoon the mixture into the prepared tin and level the top. Cover with plastic wrap and cool at room temperature for 6–8 hours, or preferably overnight.

• Once cold, peel off the plastic wrap and dust with some of the icing sugar mix. Turn over onto baking paper, peel off the plastic wrap and dust with more icing sugar. Cut into squares and roll in the sugar. Leave to dry overnight. Store for 2 weeks.

Chocolate & Coconut
Turkish Delight

preparation time : 10 minutes
cook time : 50–55 minutes, plus cooling and drying

TOOLS:

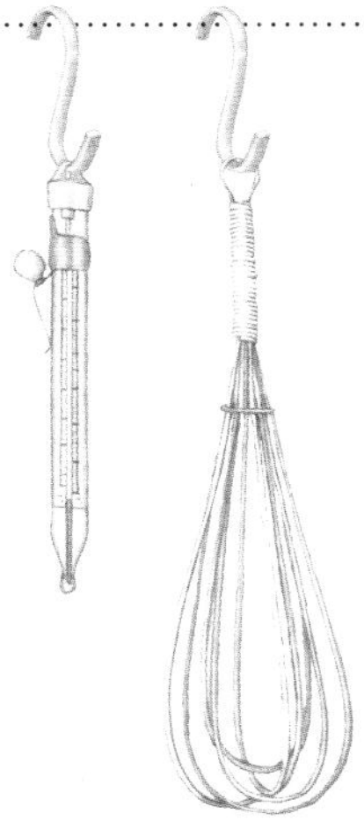

470 ml (16 fl oz) water
400 g (14 oz) granulated sugar
60 g (2 oz/½ cup) cornflour (cornstarch)
5 g (¼ oz) unsweetened (Dutch) cocoa powder
½ teaspoon cream of tartar
1 teaspoon vanilla extract
20 g (¾ oz) desiccated coconut

makes 30 *pieces*

• Line an 18 cm (7 in) square tin with plastic wrap.

• Pour 200 ml (7 fl oz) water into a saucepan and add the granulated sugar. Place over the heat and stir until the sugar has dissolved. Insert a sugar thermometer and cook until the syrup reaches 120°C (248°F).

• Meanwhile, pour the remaining water into another saucepan, add the cornflour, cocoa powder and cream of tartar and stir well ensuring that there are no lumps. Place over the heat and bring to the boil, stirring until it thickens and is smooth.

• Once the syrup has reached the correct temperature, remove from the heat and slowly add the syrup a little at a time into the cornflour mixture, whisking constantly until combined. Return to the heat and gently simmer for 30–35 minutes, stirring all the time. The mixture will turn a smooth chocolate colour and thicken. Stir in the vanilla extract and simmer for a further 5 minutes.

• Spoon the mixture into the prepared tin and level the top. Cover with more plastic wrap and cool at room temperature for 6–8 hours, or preferably overnight.

• Once cold, peel off the plastic wrap from the Turkish delight and sprinkle with desiccated coconut. Turn over onto baking paper and peel off the plastic wrap and sprinkle with more coconut. Cut into small squares and roll in more coconut. Leave to dry overnight. Store for up to 2 weeks.

7

Fudge

Soft Ball Stage

113–116°C

(235–241°F)

1 Place the sugar and water in a heavy-based saucepan.

2 Heat until the sugar has dissolved, about 5–10 minutes.

3 Insert a sugar thermometer into the saucepan and boil the mixture.

4 Clean around the sides of the pan with a damp pastry brush to avoid any crystallisation forming around the pan.

5 Once the sugar syrup reaches the correct temperature, it has reached the soft ball stage.

6 To check it has reached this stage, drop a little of the sugar syrup into a bowl of cold water – the sugar will turn into a soft pliable ball. When removed from the water it does not hold its shape and will flatten when squeezed between the fingers.

1

2

180
160
130
300
280
100
80
60
220
200
180
160
140
120
100
3

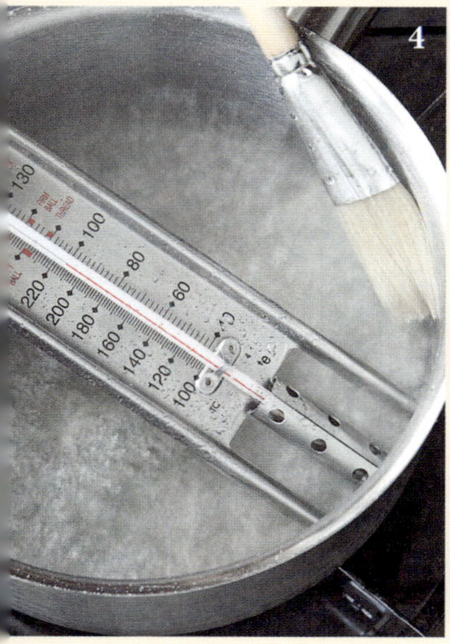
4
130
100
80
60
220
200
180
160
140
120
100

5
130
100
80
60
220
200
180
160
140
120
100

6

Vanilla Fudge

preparation time : 5 minutes
cook time : 15–20 minutes, plus cooling and setting

TOOLS:

Vegetable oil for oiling
450 g (1 lb) granulated sugar
125 ml (4 fl oz/½ cup) thick (double/heavy) cream
65 ml (2¼ fl oz) golden syrup (corn syrup)
65 ml (2¼ fl oz) evaporated milk
75 g (2¾ oz) unsalted butter
2 teaspoons vanilla extract
¼ teaspoon salt

makes 20–24 *pieces*

• Lightly oil and line the sides and base of a 450 g (1 lb) loaf (bar) tin, about 15 × 10 cm (6 × 4 in), with baking paper and set aside.

• Combine the sugar, cream, golden syrup, evaporated milk, butter, vanilla extract and salt in a heavy-based saucepan. Place over a medium heat and stir until the sugar has dissolved.

• Insert a sugar thermometer and bring the mixture to the boil. Cook until it reaches 116°C (241°F). Remove from the heat, pour the mixture into a bowl and leave to cool for 5 minutes. Using a wooden spoon, slowly beat the fudge until it cools and thickens. By beating the fudge you will get a smooth texture.

• Once thickened, spread the mixture into the prepared tin and leave to set at room temperature for at least 2–3 hours.

• Cut into pieces and store in an airtight container in the refrigerator for up to 3 weeks.

Dark Chocolate Fudge
with Candied Orange

preparation time : 10 minutes
cook time : 15–20 minutes, plus cooling and setting

TOOLS:

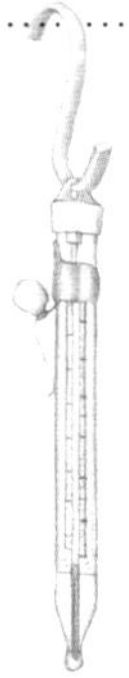

Vegetable oil for oiling
450 g (1 lb) granulated sugar
125 ml (4 fl oz/½ cup) thick (double/heavy) cream
65 ml (2¼ fl oz) golden syrup (corn syrup)
65 ml (2¼ fl oz) evaporated milk
75 g (2¾ oz) unsalted butter
70 g (2½ oz) dark chocolate (at least 70% cocoa solids), chopped
75 g (2¾ oz) Candied orange peel (page 232), chopped

makes 20–24 *pieces*

• Lightly oil and line the sides and base of a 450 g (1 lb) loaf (bar) tin, about 15 × 10 cm (6 × 4 in), with baking paper and set aside.

• Combine the sugar, cream, golden syrup, evaporated milk and butter in a heavy-based saucepan. Place over a medium heat and stir until the sugar has dissolved.

• Insert a sugar thermometer and bring the mixture to the boil. Add 40 g (1½ oz) of the dark chocolate and cook the mixture until it reaches 116°C (241°F). Remove from the heat, pour the mixture into a bowl and leave to cool for 5 minutes. Using a wooden spoon, slowly beat the fudge until it cools and thickens. By beating the fudge you will get a smooth texture.

• Stir in 50 g (1¾ oz) of the candied orange peel, then spread the mixture into the prepared tin and sprinkle the top with the remaining dark chocolate and candied peel. Leave to set at room temperature for at least 2–3 hours. Cut into pieces and store in an airtight container in the refrigerator for up to 3 weeks.

Clotted Cream Fudge
with Macadamia Nuts

preparation time : 10 minutes
cook time : 15–20 minutes, plus cooling and setting

TOOLS:

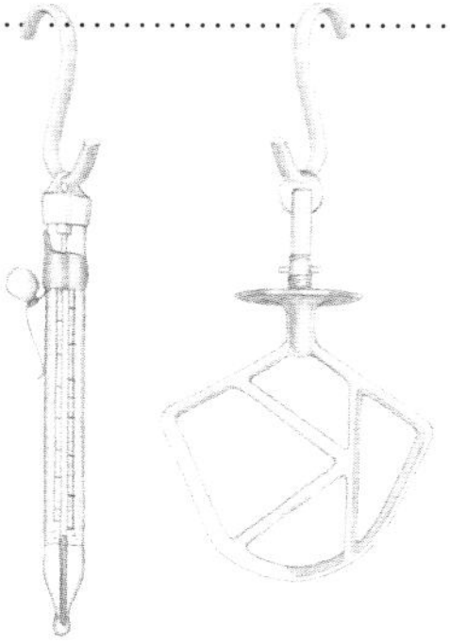

- Vegetable oil for oiling
- 250 g (9 oz) golden caster (superfine) sugar
- 200 g (7 oz) light brown sugar
- 200 g (7 oz) clotted cream
- 60 ml (2 fl oz/¼ cup) golden syrup (corn syrup)
- 75 g (2¾ oz) unsalted butter
- 1 teaspoon vanilla extract
- ¼ teaspoon salt
- 150 g (5½ oz) macadamia nuts, roughly chopped

makes 20–24 *pieces*

• Lightly oil and line the sides and base of a 450 g (1 lb) loaf (bar) tin, about 15 × 10 cm (6 × 4 in), with baking paper and set aside.

• Combine the sugars, clotted cream, golden syrup, butter, vanilla extract and salt in a heavy-based saucepan. Place over a medium heat and stir until the sugar has dissolved.

• Insert a sugar thermometer and bring the mixture to the boil. Cook the mixture until it reaches 116°C (241°F). Remove from the heat, pour the mixture into a bowl and leave to cool for 5 minutes.

• Pour the cooled mixture into a freestanding food mixer with a paddle attachment and beat on medium speed until the fudge thickens and is smooth. By beating the fudge you will get a smooth texture. Alternatively, you can use a wooden spoon to beat the mixture.

• Once thickened, stir in the chopped nuts and spread the mixture into the prepared tin. Leave to set at room temperature for at least 2–3 hours. Cut into pieces and store in an airtight container in the refrigerator for up to 3 weeks.

Pistachio & Cardamom Barfi

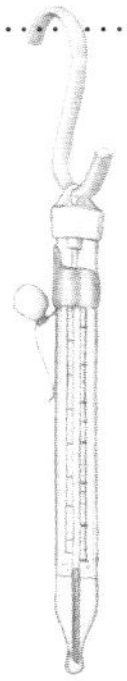

preparation time : 5 minutes
cook time : 20–25 minutes, plus cooling

TOOLS:

Vegetable oil for oiling
800 ml (27 fl oz) condensed milk
100 g (3½ oz) unsalted butter
¼ teaspoon ground cardamom
150 g (5½ oz/1 cup) pistachio nuts
Gold leaf to decorate (optional)

makes
28–30
pieces

• Lightly oil and line the sides and base of a 19 cm (7½ in) square baking tin with baking paper.

• Heat the condensed milk and butter in a saucepan over a low heat, stirring the mixture all the time to ensure that it doesn't catch or burn on the bottom of the pan. Add the ground cardamom and keep stirring for about 30–35 minutes until the mixture thickens and changes into a caramel colour. Once the mixture has thickened, insert a sugar thermometer to see if it has reached 114°C (237°F).

• Once thickened and reached the correct temperature, stir in the pistachio nuts and keep stirring for 2 minutes. Pour the mixture into the prepared tin and leave to cool at room temperature for 3–4 hours, or overnight.

• Once cooled, cut the barfi into diamonds and gild with gold leaf, if you like. Store in an airtight container for up to 3 weeks.

8

Ganache, Truffles & Chocolate Slabs

How To Temper Chocolate

Marbling

1 Place 500 g (1 lb 2 oz) dark chocolate chips in a large heatproof bowl. Place the bowl over a saucepan of gently simmering water (double-boiler) and make sure that the bowl does not touch the water.

2 Melt the chocolate and stir to ensure that all the chocolate pieces have melted. Completely melt the chocolate until it has reached 45–50°C (113–122°F). The same temperature applies to milk chocolate, but only up to 45°C (113°F) for white chocolate. The chocolate needs to reach this temperature to ensure that the fats and sugars in the chocolate have melted evenly. If the chocolate is overheated, the chocolate will be grainy and can 'seize'.

3 Pour two-thirds of the chocolate onto a marble slab and leave the remainder in the bowl over the double-boiler, off the heat.

4 Using a metal scraper or palette knife, spread the chocolate over the marble slab and gently work it by moving it back and forth. This will quickly cool down and thicken the chocolate. Cool dark chocolate to about 28–29°C (82–84°F); for milk and white chocolates cool down to 26–27°C (79–81°F).

5 Once the chocolate has cooled to the right temperature, scrape it back into the bowl with the remaining chocolate that is over the double-boiler. Now the temperature should rise to 31–32°C (88–90°F). For milk and white chocolates, they should reach 29–30°C (84–86°F). When the chocolate reaches this temperature, it has been tempered. If it does not reach this temperature, warm the water in the double-boiler and continue stirring the chocolate until it reaches the tempered temperature.

6 Mix well until smooth. The chocolate is now ready to use.

1

2

3

4

5

6

How To Temper Chocolate

Seeding

This tempering method is usually used for small batches of chocolates or if you do not have a marble slab.

1 Take 500 g (1 lb 2 oz) dark chocolate chips and place two-thirds of the chocolate into a large heatproof bowl. Place the bowl over a saucepan of gently simmering water (double-boiler) and make sure that the bowl does not touch the water.

2 Melt the chocolate and stir to ensure that all the chocolate pieces have melted. Completely melt the chocolate until it has reached 45–50°C (113–122°F). The same temperature applies to milk chocolate but only to 45°C (113°F) for white chocolate. The chocolate needs to reach this temperature to ensure that the fats and sugars in the chocolate have melted evenly. If the chocolate is overheated it might become grainy and 'seize'.

3 Add the remaining chocolate to the melted chocolate; this is called the seed.

4 Keep stirring constantly until the chocolate has melted.

5 This will cool down and thicken the chocolate to 31–32°C (88–90°F). This is the tempered temperature you are looking for. For milk and white chocolates, they should reach 29–30°C (84–86°F). If the temperature goes below this temperature, warm the water in the double-boiler and continue stirring the chocolate until it reaches the tempered temperature.

6 The chocolate should be smooth and glossy and is now ready to use.

1

2

3

4

5

6

How To

Cover Chocolate Moulds

1 Melt and temper 500 g (1 lb 2 oz) of your desired chocolate (see pages 126–9). Using a ladle, take a ladleful of the chocolate and fill the mould.

2 Tap the mould on the work surface to remove any air bubbles and to ensure that the mould is completely covered with chocolate. Turn the mould upside down to pour the chocolate back into the bowl, then tap the top of the mould to let any excess drip down into the bowl.

3 Turn the mould over and, using a scraper or palette knife, scrape off any excess chocolate. The mould should have a smooth coating of chocolate in each hole.

4 Place the mould upside down on a lined baking tray and leave to set for 15–20 minutes in a cool dry place.

5 Once the chocolate is set, fill with the desired fillings or take the chocolate out of each mould and use it as a chocolate shell or cup.

6 Pour over more melted tempered chocolate over the top of the filled mould, ensuring it is fully covered. Level the top of the mould with a scraper or palette knife and leave the chocolates to set for 3–4 hours in a cool dry place. Once set, remove the chocolates from the mould; tapping and wiggling the mould to loosen the chocolates.

1

2

3

4

5

6

Dip Chocolates

1 Melt and temper (see pages 126–9) the chocolate you want to use for dipping. To dip and coat set candies or set ganache fillings into chocolate, use chocolate dipping forks.

2 Submerge the candy with a dipping fork into the tempered chocolate.

3 Place the fork underneath the candy and lift it out of the chocolate. Move the chocolate-coated candy up and down to remove any excess chocolate around it.

4 Using another fork, scrape the bottom of the lifted chocolate.

5 Gently place the chocolate onto a lined baking tray at an angle by sliding the fork off the chocolate.

6 Repeat this with all the candies or ganache fillings and decorate as desired, then leave to set in a cool place.

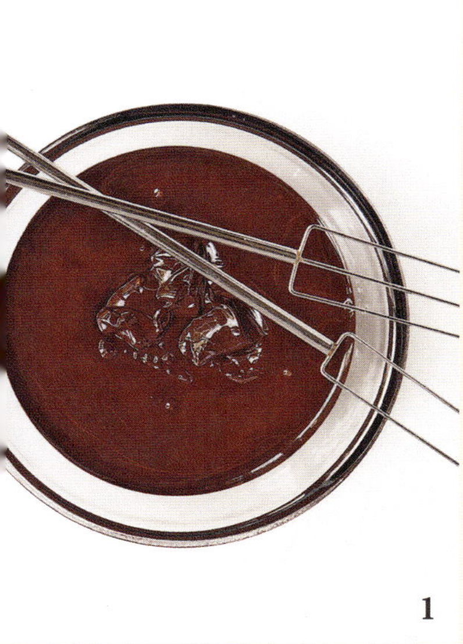

1

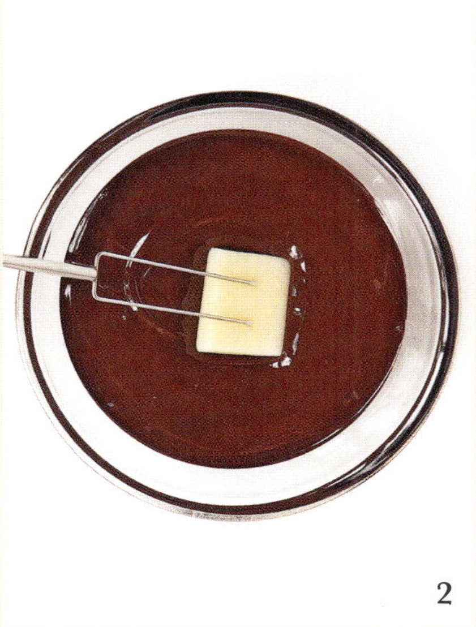

2

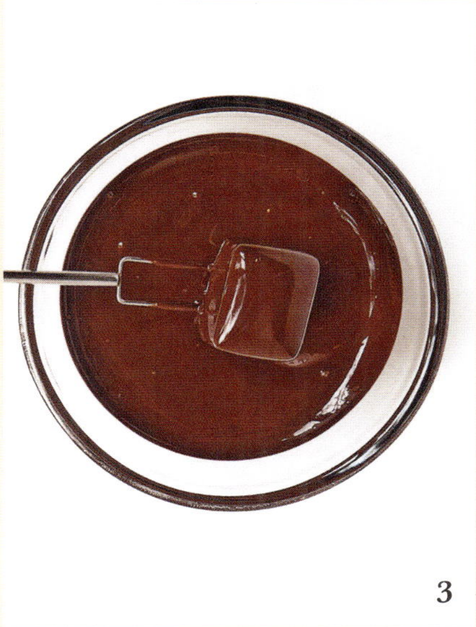

3

4

5

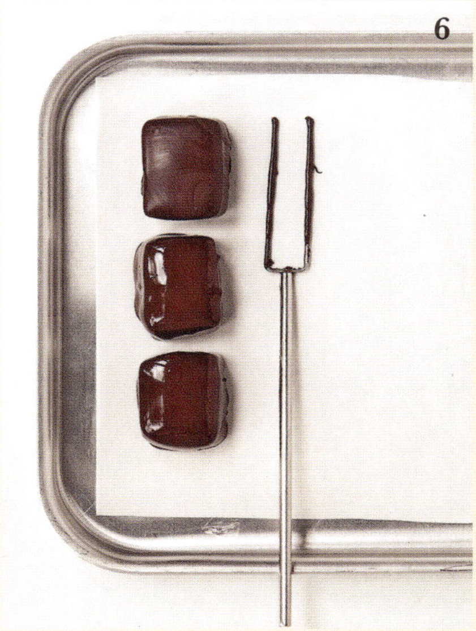

6

Basic

Dark Chocolate Ganache

1 Place 250 g (9 oz) dark chocolate chips (at least 70% cocoa solids) in a large heatproof bowl.

2 Meanwhile, bring 200 ml (7 fl oz) thick (double/heavy) cream to the boil in a saucepan, then remove the pan from the heat.

3 Pour the cream onto the chocolate.

4 Stir the cream and mix until combined.

5 Add 30 g (1 oz) butter, a cube at a time, stirring after each addition until the butter is well mixed.

6 The ganache should be smooth and glossy. Leave to set for at least 4 hours before making into truffles, or the mixture/ganache can be used to glaze cakes and as a filling for chocolates.

1

2

3

4

5

6

White Chocolate & Coffee

Ganache Chocolates

preparation time : 30 minutes
cook time : 5 minutes, plus setting

TOOLS:

500 g (1 lb 2 oz) white chocolate chips
350 ml (12 fl oz) thick (double/heavy) cream
50 g (1¾ oz) unsalted butter, cubed
2 teaspoons instant espresso powder
500 g (1 lb 2 oz) dark chocolate (at least 70% cocoa solids), tempered (see pages 126–9) for dipping
Coffee beans to decorate

makes
40
pieces

- Line two 30 × 21 cm (12 × 8¼ in) baking trays with baking paper.
- Place the white chocolate in a large heatproof bowl.
- Meanwhile, heat the cream in a saucepan and bring to the boil. Pour the cream onto the chocolate and mix well. Add the butter, a cube at a time, and mix until fully combined and smooth.
- Divide the mixture into 2 bowls and in one of them add the espresso powder and stir well. Set 2 tablespoons of the white chocolate ganache aside.
- Pour the ganaches onto the prepared trays. You will have a thin layer of ganache in each tray. Leave the ganache to set for about 30 minutes.
- Warm the reserved white chocolate ganache slightly if set. Using a pastry brush, paint a thin layer of the reserved ganache onto the coffee ganache. Invert the white chocolate ganache over the coffee ganache and sandwich together pressing gently and peel away the baking paper. Leave to set overnight in a cool dry place.
- Cut the ganache into squares and dip into tempered dark chocolate (see page 132). Decorate each with a coffee bean and leave to set for at least 4 hours. Store in a cool dry place for up to 5 days.

Chocolate & Peanut

Ganache Chocolates

preparation time : 25–30 minutes
cook time : 5 minutes, plus setting

TOOLS:

100 g (3½ oz) unsalted peanuts, roasted

500 g (1 lb 2 oz) milk chocolate chips

400 ml (13½ fl oz) thick (double/heavy) cream

50 g (1¾ oz) unsalted butter, cubed

½ teaspoon fine sea salt

500 g (1 lb 2 oz) dark chocolate (at least 70% cocoa solids), tempered (see pages 126–9)

Chopped peanuts to decorate

makes
40
pieces

• Line a 30 × 21 cm (12 × 8¼ in) baking tray with baking paper.

• Blitz the peanuts in a food processor until finely chopped. Place the milk chocolate chips in a large heatproof bowl.

• Meanwhile, heat the cream in a saucepan and bring to the boil, then pour the cream onto the chocolate and mix well. Add the butter, a cube at a time, and mix until combined and smooth. Stir in the peanuts and sea salt until well combined. Pour the ganache onto the prepared tray and leave to set overnight.

• Cut the ganache into squares and dip into the tempered dark chocolate (see page 132). Decorate with chopped peanuts and leave to set for at least 4 hours. Store in a cool dry place for up to 5 days.

Bitter Orange
Ganache Chocolates

preparation time : 25–30 minutes
cook time : 5 minutes, plus setting

TOOLS:

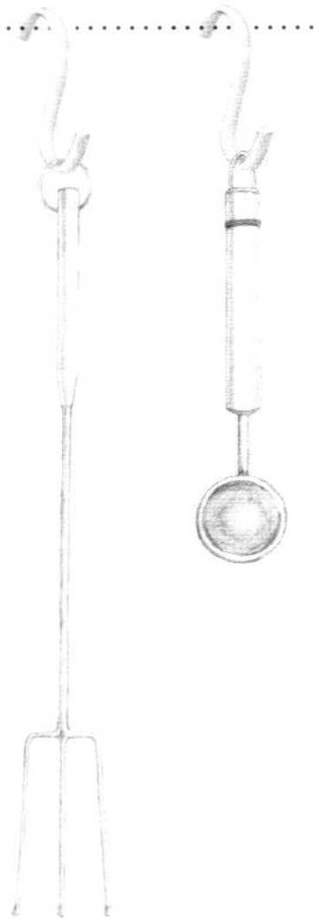

50 g (1¾ oz) Candied orange peel (page 232), plus extra sliced candied orange peel to decorate

500 g (1 lb 2 oz) dark chocolate chips (70% cocoa solids)

400 ml (13½ fl oz) orange juice

50 g (1¾ oz) unsalted butter, cubed

500 g (1 lb 2 oz) dark chocolate (at least 70% cocoa solids), tempered (see pages 126–9)

makes
40
pieces

• Line a 30 × 21 cm (12 × 8¼ in) rectangular tin with baking paper.

• Finely chop the candied orange peel and set aside. Place the chocolate chips in a large heatproof bowl.

• Meanwhile, heat the orange juice in a saucepan and bring to the boil. Pour the orange juice onto the chocolate and mix well. Add the butter, a cube at a time, and mix until fully combined and smooth. Stir in the chopped candied orange peel until well combined. Pour the ganache onto the prepared tray and leave to set overnight.

• Using a melon baller, scoop rounds or cut the ganache into squares and dip into tempered dark chocolate.

• Decorate with the extra sliced candied orange peel and leave to set for at least 4 hours in a cool dry place. Store in a cool dry place for up to 5 days.

Chocolate Cups

with Lavender, Matcha & Strawberry Ganache

TOOLS:

preparation time : 1 hour

cook time : 5–10 minutes, plus cooling and setting

45 chocolate cup shells (see page 130)

LAVENDER GANACHE

80 ml (2½ fl oz/⅓ cup) thick (double/heavy) cream

1 teaspoon dried lavender flowers, lightly bruised

150 g (5½ oz) white chocolate chips

15 g (½ oz) unsalted butter

1 drop of violet food colouring

MATCHA TEA GANACHE

150 g (5½ oz) white chocolate chips

80 ml (2½ fl oz/⅓ cup) thick (double/heavy) cream

1 teaspoon matcha tea

15 g (½ oz) unsalted butter

1 drop of green food colouring

STRAWBERRY GANACHE

150 g (5½ oz) white chocolate chips

80 ml (2½ fl oz/⅓ cup) thick (double/heavy) cream

20 g (¾ oz) strawberry jam

15 g (½ oz) unsalted butter

1 drop of pink food colouring

makes
45
cups

• For the lavender ganache, bring the cream and lavender to the boil in a saucepan, then remove from the heat and let the cream infuse for 1 minute.

• Place the chocolate in a heatproof bowl and strain over the infused cream. Stir until combined. Add the butter and colouring and mix until smooth. Cool.

• For the matcha tea ganache, place the chocolate in a heatproof bowl. Bring the cream to the boil in a saucepan, then pour over the chocolate. Add the matcha tea and stir until well combined. Add the butter and food colouring and mix well until combined and smooth. Leave to cool.

• For the strawberry ganache, place the chocolate in a heatproof bowl. Bring the cream to the boil in a saucepan, then pour over the chocolate. Add the strawberry jam and stir until well combined. Add the butter and food colouring and mix until smooth. Leave to cool.

TO ASSEMBLE THE CUPS

• Once all the flavoured ganaches have cooled but not set, place them into piping bags with star nozzles. Pipe the ganaches into the prepared chocolate cup shells until they resemble little mini cupcakes. Leave to set at room temperature for at least 2 hours. Store in a cool dry place for up to 5 days.

Basic Truffles

preparation time : 30 minutes, plus setting
cook time : none

TOOLS:

50 g ($1^{3}/_{4}$ oz) unsweetened (Dutch) cocoa powder, sifted, plus extra for dusting

1 batch of set Dark chocolate ganache (page 134)

100 g ($3^{1}/_{2}$ oz) dark chocolate (at least 70% cocoa solids), melted

makes
40
truffles

• Line a baking tray with baking paper.

• Lightly dust your hands with cocoa powder, then take heaped teaspoons of the ganache and roll it into balls.

• Place the remaining cocoa powder in a shallow dish or tray.

• Half dip the truffle into the melted chocolate and roll in your palms ensuring that the melted chocolate is covering the truffle. Roll in the cocoa powder, shaking off any excess powder, then place onto the prepared baking tray and leave to set in a cool dry place for about 1 hour. Store in a cool dry place for up to 5 days.

Chilli & Cinnamon
Truffles

preparation time : 20–30 minutes
cook time : 5 minutes, plus setting

50 g (1¾ oz) unsweetened (Dutch) cocoa powder, sifted, plus extra for dusting
2 teaspoons chilli flakes
1¼ teaspoons ground cinnamon
250 g (9 oz) dark chocolate chips (70% cocoa solids)
200 ml (7 fl oz) thick (double/heavy) cream
4 small dried chillies, crumbled
30 g (1 oz) unsalted butter, cubed
100 g (3½ oz) dark chocolate (at least 70% cocoa solids), melted

TOOLS:

makes
40
truffles

• Line a baking tray with baking paper.

• In a bowl, mix together the cocoa powder, chilli flakes and 1 teaspoon of ground cinnamon and place in a shallow dish or tray.

• Place the chocolate chips in a large heatproof bowl.

• Meanwhile, bring the cream and crumbled dried chillies to the boil in a saucepan. Remove from the heat and leave to infuse for 1 minute.

• Strain and pour the cream onto the chocolate and mix well. Add the remaining ground cinnamon and butter, a cube at a time, and mix until fully combined and smooth. Leave the ganache to set for at least 4 hours before making into truffles.

• Lightly dust your hands with cocoa powder, then take heaped teaspoons of the ganache and roll it into balls. Half dip the truffles into the melted chocolate and roll in your palms ensuring that the melted chocolate is covering the truffle. Roll in the cocoa powder–chilli mixture, shaking off any excess then place on the prepared baking tray and leave to set in a cool dry place for about 1 hour. Store in a cool dry place for up to 5 days.

Spiced Latte & Coconut
Truffles

preparation time : 30 minutes
cook time : 5–10 minutes, plus setting

50 g (1¾ oz) desiccated coconut
250 g (9 oz) white chocolate chips
180 ml (6 fl oz) thick (double/heavy) cream
2 cardamom pods, bruised
2 cloves
1 strip of orange zest
25 g (1 oz) unsalted butter, cubed
100 g (3½ oz) white chocolate chips, melted
Icing (confectioners') sugar for dusting

TOOLS:

makes
40
truffles

- Line a baking tray with baking paper.
- Place the desiccated coconut in a shallow dish or tray. Place the white chocolate chips in a large heatproof bowl.
- Meanwhile, bring the cream, bruised cardamom, cloves and orange rind to the boil in a saucepan. Remove from the heat and leave to infuse for 2 minutes.
- Strain and pour the cream onto the chocolate and mix well. Add the butter, a cube at a time, and mix until fully combined and smooth. Leave the ganache to set for at least 4 hours before making into truffles.
- Lightly dust your hands with icing sugar, then take heaped teaspoons of the ganache and roll it into balls. Half dip the truffle into the melted chocolate and roll in your palms ensuring that the melted chocolate is covering the truffle. Roll in the desiccated coconut, shaking off any excess then place on the prepared baking tray and leave to set in a cool dry place for about 1 hour. Store in a cool dry place for up to 5 days.

Cherry Truffles

preparation time : 30 minutes
cook time : 5 minutes, plus setting

TOOLS:

250 g (9 oz) dark chocolate chips (70% cocoa solids)
200 ml (7 fl oz) thick (double/heavy) cream
30 g (1 oz) unsalted butter, cubed
75 g (2³/₄ oz) dried cherries
20 g (³/₄ oz) freeze-dried cherries, finely chopped
Unsweetened (Dutch) cocoa powder for dusting
100 g (3¹/₂ oz) dark chocolate (at least 70% cocoa solids), melted

makes 40 *truffles*

• Line a baking tray with baking paper. Place the chocolate chips in a large heatproof bowl.

• Meanwhile, bring the cream to the boil in a saucepan. Remove from the heat and pour the cream onto the chocolate and mix well. Add the butter, a cube at a time, and mix until fully combined and smooth, then stir in the dried cherries. Leave the ganache to set for at least 4 hours before making into truffles.

• Place the freeze-dried cherries into a shallow bowl or tray.

• Once the ganache has set, lightly dust your hands with cocoa powder, then take heaped teaspoons of the ganache and roll into balls. Half dip the truffle into the melted chocolate and roll in your palms ensuring that the melted chocolate is covering the truffle. Roll into the freeze-dried cherries and place onto the baking tray.

• Leave to set in a cool dry place for about 1 hour. Store in a cool dry place for up to 5 days.

Mint & Pistachio

Truffles

preparation time : 30 minutes
cook time : 5 minutes, plus setting

TOOLS

75 g (2¾ oz) pistachio nuts, toasted
250 g (9 oz) dark chocolate chips (70% cocoa solids)
200 ml (7 fl oz) thick (double/heavy) cream
10 g (¼ oz) fresh mint, torn
30 g (1 oz) unsalted butter, cubed
Unsweetened (Dutch) cocoa powder for dusting
100 g (3½ oz) dark chocolate (at least 70% cocoa solids), melted

makes
40
truffles

• Line a baking tray with baking paper.

• Finely chop the pistachio nuts and place into a shallow dish or tray. Place the chocolate chips in a large heatproof bowl.

• Meanwhile, bring the cream and torn mint to the boil in a saucepan. Remove from the heat and leave to infuse for 2 minutes.

• Strain and pour the cream onto the chocolate and mix well. Add the butter, a cube at a time, and mix until fully combined and smooth. Leave the ganache to set for at least 4 hours before making into truffles.

• Lightly dust your hands with cocoa powder, then take heaped teaspoons of the ganache and roll into balls. Half dip the truffle into the melted chocolate and roll in your palms ensuring that the melted chocolate is covering the truffle. Roll into the chopped pistachio nuts, shaking off any excess, then place on the prepared baking tray and leave to set in a cool dry place for about 1 hour. Store in a cool dry place for up to 5 days.

Chocolate Lollipops

with Toppings & Sprinkles

preparation time : 30–35 minutes, plus setting
cook time : none

150 g ($5\frac{1}{2}$ oz) white chocolate chips, tempered (see pages 126–9)

150 g ($5\frac{1}{2}$ oz) pink chocolate melts (buttons), tempered (see pages 126–9)

TOPPINGS

2 tablespoons toasted black and white sesame seeds

3 chocolate or Oreo cookies, crushed

50 g ($1\frac{3}{4}$ oz) Honeycomb (page 26), finely chopped

2 tablespoons sugar sprinkles

makes 12 *lollipops*

- Line 2 large baking trays with baking paper and draw circles of about 4 cm ($1\frac{1}{2}$ in) in diameter all over the paper. Place a spoonful of chocolate within the circles, making them into discs, then place a lollipop stick firmly into the chocolate discs. Alternatively, if you have a lollipop mould, fill them up and insert the lollipop sticks.
- Sprinkle with different toppings and leave to set in a cool dry place for at least 1 hour. Store in a cool dry place for up to a week.

NOTE:
You can buy the coloured and flavoured chocolates from specialist sugarcraft shops or from supermarkets.

Chocolate Florentines

Chocolate Discs with Luxury Fruit & Nuts

preparation time : 30 minutes, plus setting
cook time : none

- 20 g (3/4 oz) pepitas (pumpkin seeds)
- 20 g (3/4 oz) sunflower seeds
- 20 g (3/4 oz) flaked almonds, toasted
- 20 g (3/4 oz) pistachio nuts, toasted
- 20 g (3/4 oz) whole hazelnuts, toasted
- 30 g (1 oz) dried apricots
- 30 g (1 oz) dried cranberries
- 40 g (1 1/2 oz) dried figs
- 30 g (1 oz) Candied orange peel (page 232)
- 30 g (1 oz) candied ginger
- 300 g (10 1/2 oz) dark chocolate (at least 70% cocoa solids), melted

makes
12
florentines

• Line a large baking tray with baking paper and draw circles of about 4 cm (1 1/2 in) in diameter.

• Roughly chop the nuts, and cut the dried fruits into small pieces.

• Place a spoonful of chocolate within the circles on the lined baking tray making them into discs. Place the fruit, nut and seeds onto the chocolate discs, pressing gently into the chocolate, then leave to set in a cool dry place for at least 1 hour. Store in a cool dry place for up to a week.

Praline & Wafer

Chocolate Bars

preparation time : 30–35 minutes, plus cooling and setting
cook time : none

TOOLS:

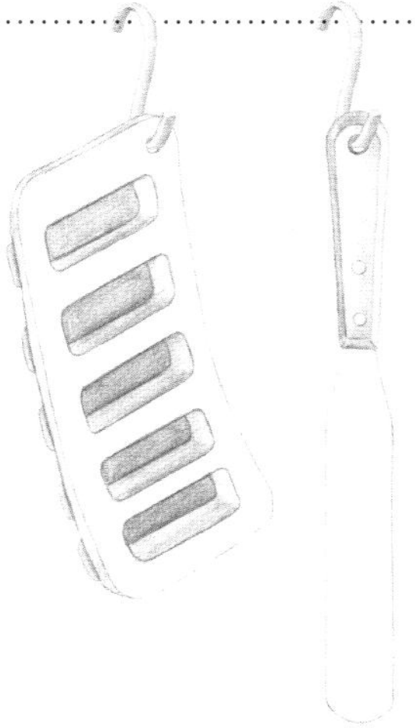

500 g (1 lb 2 oz) dark chocolate (at least 70% cocoa solids), tempered (see pages 126–9)

100 g (3½ oz) milk chocolate chips

100 g (3½ oz) praline paste (see page 216)

60 g (2 oz/2 cups) rice bubbles (rice crispies), roughly crushed

makes
8
bars

- Line a baking tray with baking paper.
- Pour the tempered chocolate into a mould, tap to remove any air bubbles then pour the chocolate back into the bowl. Scrape the top of any excess.
- Turn the mould over, place onto the prepared baking tray and leave to set for 15–20 minutes in a cool dry place.
- Melt the milk chocolate in a heatproof bowl set over a saucepan of gently simmering water. Make sure the bottom of the bowl doesn't touch the water. Once melted, add the praline paste, remove from the double-boiler and leave to cool.
- Once cooled, stir in the rice bubbles and mix well. Spoon some praline mixture into the set moulds, filling almost to the top. Level it off with a palette knife. Pour more tempered chocolate over the top of the praline filling and scrape along the top to ensure it is sealed with chocolate. Leave to set in a cool dry place for at least 3–4 hours.
- Once set, gently tap the chocolate bars out of the moulds. Store in a cool dry place for up to a week.

Doughnut-shaped

Praline-Filled Chocolates

preparation time : 35–40 minutes, plus cooling and setting

cook time : none

TOOLS:

500 g (1 lb 2 oz) dark chocolate (at least 70% cocoa solids), tempered (see pages 126–9)

100 g (3½ oz) milk chocolate chips

100 g (3½ oz) praline paste (see page 216)

30 g (1 oz) hazelnuts, finely chopped

50 g (1¾ oz) pink chocolate melts (buttons)

makes
18
chocolates

• Line a baking tray with baking paper.

• Pour the tempered chocolate into a mini doughnut mould, then tap to remove air bubbles and pour the chocolate back into the bowl. Scrape the top of any excess.

• Turn the mould over, place on the prepared tray and leave to set for 15–20 minutes in a cool dry place.

• Melt the 100 g (3½ oz) milk chocolate in a heatproof bowl set over a saucepan of gently simmering water. Make sure the bottom of the bowl doesn't touch the water. Once melted, add the praline paste, remove from the double-boiler and leave to cool.

• Once cooled, stir in the chopped hazelnuts and mix well. Spoon some praline mixture into the set moulds, filling almost to the top and level it off with a palette knife.

• Pour more tempered chocolate over the top of the praline filling and scrape along the top to ensure it is sealed with chocolate. Leave to set for at least 3–4 hours in a cool dry place.

• Once set, gently tap the chocolate doughnuts out of the moulds and place onto a sheet of baking paper.

• Melt the pink chocolate melts and fill a small piping bag. Snip the end to get a fine hole and drizzle onto the chocolate doughnuts. Leave to set for at least 1 hour. Store in a cool dry place for up to a week.

Peanut Butter
& Jelly Cups

preparation time : 30 minutes
cook time : 15–20 minutes, plus cooling and setting

TOOLS:

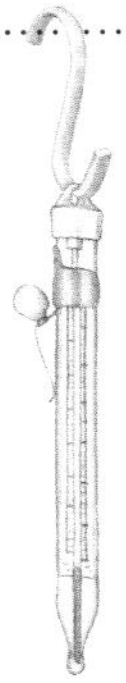

45 chocolate cup shells (see page 130)
200 g (7 oz) smooth peanut butter
50 g (1¾ oz) icing (confectioners') sugar

JELLY
200 ml (7 fl oz) blueberry purée
100 g (3½ oz) preserving sugar

makes
45
jelly cups

• For the jelly, place the purée and sugar together in a saucepan then place over the heat and stir until the sugar has dissolved. Insert a sugar thermometer, bring to the boil and cook until the mixture reaches 120°C (248°F). Remove from the heat, place in a bowl and leave to cool.

• Meanwhile, place the peanut butter and icing sugar in a bowl and stir to make a paste.

• Fill a third of the chocolate cups with the peanut butter mixture, then spoon a third of the jelly on top. Leave to set in a cool dry place for at least 30 minutes. Once set, fill with another third of peanut butter on the top.

• The cups are ready to eat immediately. Store in a cool dry place for up to a week.

Crunchy Mint Thins

preparation time : 30 minutes, plus setting
cook time : none

TOOLS

100 g (3½ oz) hardened Dry caramel (page 214), broken into pieces

1 teaspoon mint flavouring oil

250 g (9 oz) dark chocolate (at least 70% cocoa solids), tempered (see pages 126–9)

makes
350 g
(12½ oz)

• Line a large baking tray with a silicone mat or baking paper.

• Blitz the caramel pieces in a food processor until you have a sandy crumb. Add the mint flavouring to the melted chocolate and mix well.

• Pour the melted chocolate onto the prepared baking tray and spread the chocolate thinly. Sprinkle the caramel crumbs over the chocolate and level with a palette knife.

• Place another silicone mat or baking paper over the top of the chocolate and place another baking tray or tray on the top to weigh it down. Leave to set in a cool dry place for at least 2 hours.

• Once set, remove the baking tray and peel off the mat from the chocolate thins. Break into shards. Store in an airtight container in a cool dry place for up to a week.

Black & White Sesame Thins

preparation time : 30 minutes
cook time : 5 minutes, plus cooling and setting

TOOLS:

20 g (3/4 oz) white sesame seeds
20 g (3/4 oz) black sesame seeds
200 g (7 oz) white chocolate, tempered (see pages 126–9)

makes
240 g
(8 1/2 oz)

- Line a baking tray with a silicone mat or baking paper.
- Lightly toast the sesame seeds in a frying pan and leave to cool.
- Once cooled, mix both the white and black sesame seeds into the tempered white chocolate and mix well. Pour the melted chocolate onto the prepared baking tray and spread the chocolate thinly with a palette knife.
- Place another silicone mat or baking paper over the top of the chocolate and place another baking tray or tray on the top to weigh it down. Leave to set in a cool dry place for at least 2 hours.
- Once set, remove the baking tray and peel off the mat from the chocolate thins. Break into shards. Store in a cool dry place for up to a week.

Basic Soft Caramel

Chocolate Filling

preparation time : 20–25 minutes
cook time : 10–15 minutes, plus cooling and setting

TOOLS:

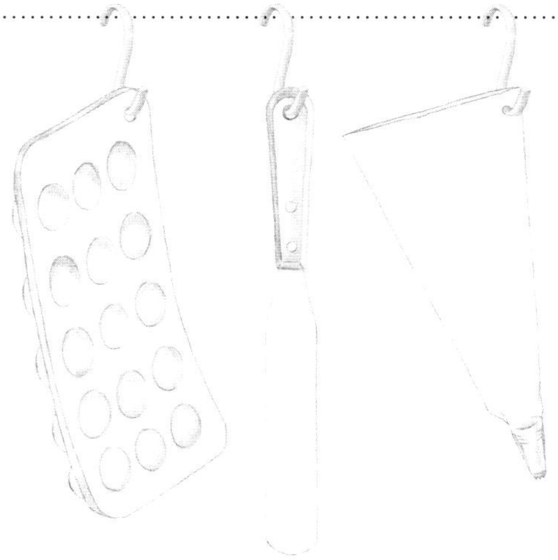

200 g (7 oz) caster (superfine) sugar
30 ml (1 fl oz) liquid glucose
125 ml (4 fl oz/½ cup) thick (double/heavy) cream
1 teaspoon vanilla extract
150 g (5½ oz) unsalted butter, cubed
500 g (1 lb 2 oz) milk chocolate, tempered (see pages 126–9)

makes
40
pieces

• Place the sugar and liquid glucose in a heavy-based saucepan and heat over a medium heat until the sugar melts and forms an amber coloured caramel.

• Meanwhile, heat the cream and vanilla extract together in a saucepan. Bring to the boil and remove from the heat. Add the cream to the caramel mixture and mix well until combined. Remove from the heat and add the butter, a cube at a time, and mix the caramel well. Leave to cool in a cool dry place for about 20 minutes.

• Use the tempered milk chocolate to cover a silicone heart-shaped chocolate mould (see page 130).

• Put the cooled caramel into a piping bag and fill the chocolate moulds three-quarters full with the caramel. Leave to set for at least 15 minutes.

• Pour more tempered chocolate over the caramel filled chocolates (see page 130) and leave to set in a cool dry place for at least 2 hours. Unmould and store in an airtight container in a cool dry place for up to a week.

Basil-infused Caramel
Chocolates

preparation time : 20–25 minutes
cook time : 10–15 minutes, plus cooling and setting

125 ml (4 fl oz/½ cup) thick (double/heavy) cream
10 g (¼ oz) basil, torn roughly
200 g (7 oz) caster (superfine) sugar
30 ml (1 fl oz) liquid glucose
150 g (5½ oz) unsalted butter, cubed
500 g (1 lb 2 oz) dark chocolate (at least 70% cocoa solids), tempered (see pages 126–9)

TOOLS

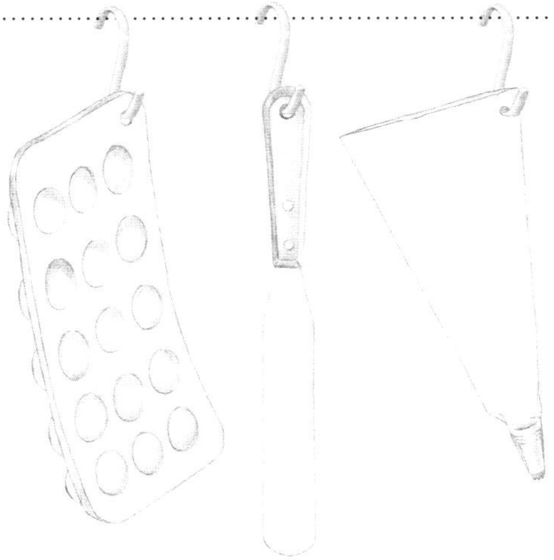

makes 40 *pieces*

• Heat the double cream and basil together in a saucepan. Bring to the boil and remove from the heat. Leave to infuse for a few minutes.

• Meanwhile, place the sugar and liquid glucose in a heavy-based saucepan and heat over a medium heat until the sugar melts and forms an amber coloured caramel.

• Strain the cream into the caramel mixture and mix until well combined. Remove from the heat and add the butter, a cube at a time, and mix the caramel well. Leave to cool in a cool dry place for about 20 minutes.

• Use the tempered dark chocolate to cover silicone chocolate mould shapes of your choice (see page 130).

• Put the cooled caramel into a piping bag and fill the chocolate mould three-quarters full with the caramel, then leave to set for at least 15 minutes.

• Pour more tempered chocolate over the caramel-filled chocolates (see page 130) and leave to set in a cool dry place for at least 2 hours. Unmould and store in an airtight container in a cool dry place for up to a week.

Salted Butter Caramel
Chocolates

preparation time : 20–25 minutes
cook time : 10–15 minutes, plus cooling and setting

TOOLS:

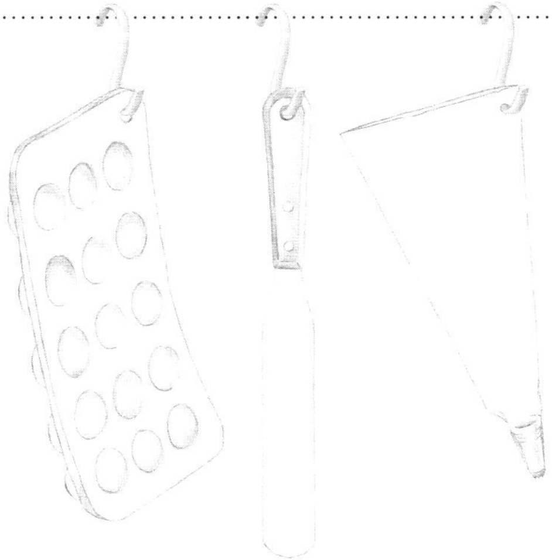

200 g (7 oz) caster (superfine) sugar
30 ml (1 fl oz) liquid glucose
125 ml (4 fl oz/½ cup) thick (double/heavy) cream
Seeds from 1 vanilla pod
150 g (5½ oz) salted butter, cubed
500 g (1 lb 2 oz) dark chocolate (at least 70% cocoa solids), tempered (see pages 126–9)

makes
40
pieces

• Place the sugar and liquid glucose in a heavy-based saucepan and heat over a medium heat until the sugar melts and forms an amber coloured caramel.

• Meanwhile, heat the double cream and vanilla seeds together in a saucepan. Bring to the boil and remove from the heat. Add the cream into the caramel mixture and mix well until combined. Remove from the heat and add the butter, a cube at a time, and mix the caramel well. Leave to cool in a cool dry place for about 20 minutes.

• Use the tempered dark chocolate to cover silicone mould shapes of your choice (see page 130).

• Put the cooled caramel into a piping bag and fill the mould shape three-quarters full with the caramel, then leave to set for at least 15 minutes.

• Pour more tempered chocolate over the caramel filled chocolates (see page 130) and leave to set in a cool dry place for at least 2 hours. Unmould and store in an airtight container in a cool dry place for up to a week.

Vanilla & Maple Syrup
Caramel Chocolates

preparation time : 20–25 minutes
cook time : 10–15 minutes, plus cooling and setting

200 g (7 oz) caster (superfine) sugar
30 ml (1 fl oz) liquid glucose
60 ml (2 fl oz/¼ cup) maple syrup
70 ml (2¼ fl oz) thick (double/heavy) cream
Seeds from 1 vanilla pod
100 g (3½ oz) unsalted butter, cubed
500 g (1 lb 2 oz) dark chocolate (at least 70% cocoa solids), tempered (see pages 126–9)

TOOLS:

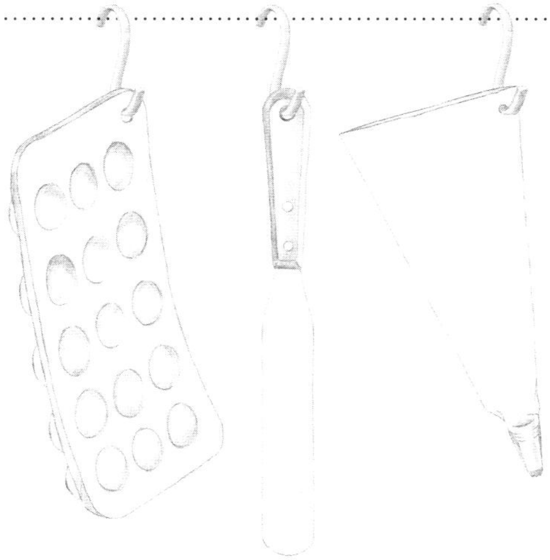

makes 40 *pieces*

• Place the sugar and liquid glucose in a heavy-based saucepan and heat over a medium heat until the sugar melts and forms an amber coloured caramel.

• Meanwhile, heat the maple syrup, double cream and vanilla seeds together in a saucepan. Bring to the boil and remove from the heat. Add the cream into the caramel mixture and mix well until combined. Remove from the heat and add the butter, a cube at a time, and mix the caramel well. Leave to cool in a cool dry place for about 20 minutes.

• Use the tempered dark chocolate to cover silicone mould shapes of your choice (see page 130).

• Put the cooled caramel into a piping bag and fill each mould three-quarters full with the caramel, then leave to set for at least 15 minutes.

• Pour more tempered chocolate over the caramel filled chocolates (see page 130) and leave to set in a cool dry place for at least 2 hours. Unmould and store in an airtight container in a cool dry place for up to a week.

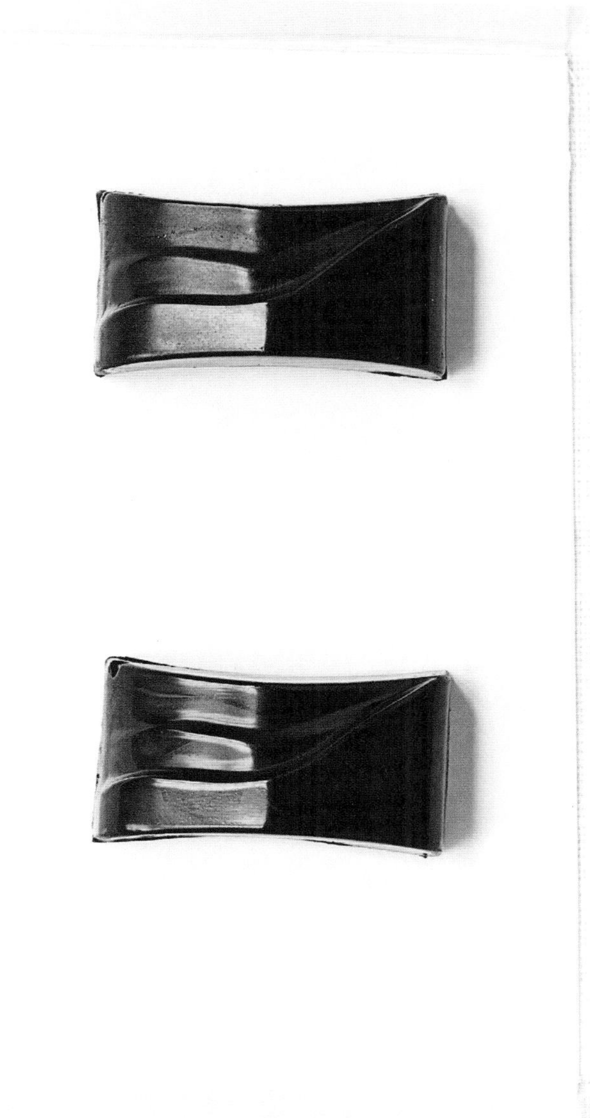

Lemon & Orange Blossom

Caramel Chocolates

preparation time : 20–25 minutes
cook time : 20–25 minutes, plus cooling and setting

TOOLS

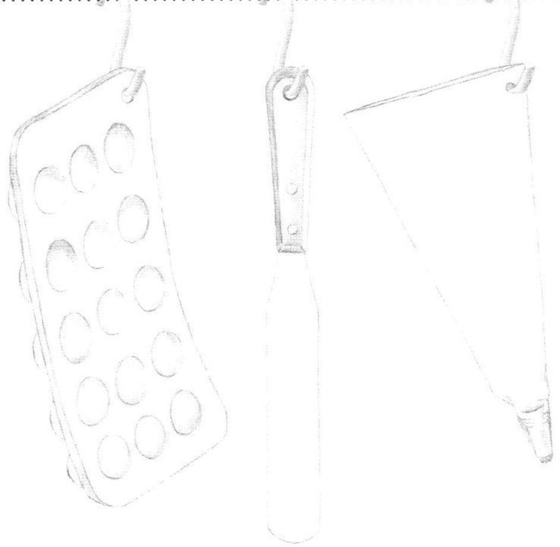

60 ml (2 fl oz/¼ cup) lemon juice
60 ml (2 fl oz/¼ cup) orange juice
200 g (7 oz) caster (superfine) sugar
30 ml (1 fl oz) liquid glucose
80 ml (2½ fl oz/⅓ cup) thick (double/heavy) cream
1 tablespoon orange blossom water
100 g (3½ oz) unsalted butter, cubed
500 g (1 lb 2 oz) white chocolate, tempered (see pages 126–9)

makes
40
pieces

• Bring the 2 juices to the boil in a small saucepan and reduce them by half.

• Place the sugar and liquid glucose in a heavy-based saucepan and heat over a medium heat until the sugar melts and forms an amber coloured caramel.

• Meanwhile, heat the cream in another small saucepan. Add the cream into the caramel and mix well. Stir in the reduced juices and orange blossom water and mix well. Remove the pan from the heat and stir in the butter, a little at a time, and mix the caramel well. Leave to cool in a cool dry place for about 20 minutes.

• Use the tempered white chocolate to cover silicone mould shapes of your choice (see page 130).

• Put the cooled caramel into a piping bag and fill the moulds three-quarters full with the caramel, then leave to set for at least 15 minutes.

• Pour more tempered chocolate over the caramel filled chocolates (see page 130) and leave to set in a cool dry place for at least 2 hours. Unmould and store in an airtight container in a cool dry place for up to a week.

Sea Salt & Caramel

Chocolate Slab

preparation time : 30 minutes, plus setting
cook time : none

TOOLS:

400 g (14 oz) milk or dark chocolate (at least 70% cocoa solids), tempered (see pages 126–9)

100 g (3½ oz) caramel candy (see page 214), roughly chopped

2 teaspoons sea salt flakes

makes
2 *large or* 4 *small*
bars

• Pour the chocolate into the slab moulds and ensure that they are fully covered, tapping to eliminate any air bubbles. Using a scraper or palette knife, scrape the top to remove any excess chocolate and to level the surface.

• Gently dot the caramel randomly onto the chocolate slab and sprinkle with the sea salt flakes. Leave to set in a cool dry place for at least 4 hours, or overnight.

• Slowly loosen the chocolate from the moulds. Store in a cool dry place for up to a week.

Banoffee Chocolate Slab

preparation time : 30 minutes, plus setting
cook time : none

60 g (2 oz) Vanilla fudge (page 116)

400 g (14 oz) milk chocolate, tempered (see pages 126–9)

50 g (1¾ oz) banana chips

30 g (1 oz) digestive (sweet wholemeal) cookies, crushed

TOOLS:

makes
2 *large or* 4 *small*
bars

- Cut the vanilla fudge into small pieces and set aside.
- Pour the tempered chocolate into the slab moulds and ensure that they are fully covered, tapping to eliminate any air bubbles. Using a scraper or palette knife, scrape the top to remove any excess chocolate and to level the surface.
- Gently dot the banana chips, fudge and crushed cookies randomly onto the chocolate slab. Leave to set in a cool dry place for at least 4 hours, or overnight.
- Slowly loosen the chocolate from the moulds. Store in a cool dry place for up to a week.

Rocky Road

Chocolate Slab

preparation time : 15 minutes
cook time : 5 minutes, plus cooling and setting

Vegetable oil for oiling
30 g (1 oz) pistachio nuts
150 g (5½ oz) rich tea (plain sweet) cookies
100 g (3½ oz) marshmallows (see page 86)
50 g (1¾ oz) glacé cherries
300 g (10½ oz) dark chocolate chips (70% cocoa solids)
125 g (4½ oz) unsalted butter
45 ml (1½ fl oz) golden syrup (corn syrup)

makes
16
squares

• Oil and line the base and sides of a 19 cm (7½ in) square baking tin with baking paper.

• Lightly toast the pistachio nuts in a frying pan and leave to cool. Break the cookies into small pieces, cut the marshmallows into quarters and the glacé cherries in halves.

• Heat the chocolate, butter and golden syrup together in a saucepan over a low heat. Gently melt the chocolate and butter and mix until well combined. Remove from the heat and add the nuts, cookies, marshmallows and cherries.

• Spoon the mixture into the prepared tin and leave to set in the refrigerator for at least 4 hours, or overnight.

• Once set, remove from the tin and cut into squares or rectangles. Store in an airtight container in a cool dry place for up to a week.

Strawberry & Pink Peppercorn
Chocolate Slab

preparation time : 30 minutes, plus setting
cook time : none

TOOLS:

50 g (1¾ oz) pink strawberry chocolate, melted
400 g (14 oz) white chocolate, tempered (see pages 126–9)
20 g (¾ oz) dried strawberries
1 tablespoon pink peppercorns

makes
2 *large or* 4 *small*
bars

• Gently stir the pink strawberry chocolate into the white chocolate, leaving swirls to create a marble effect. Pour the chocolate into the slab moulds and ensure that they are fully covered, tapping to eliminate any air bubbles. Using a scraper or palette knife, scrape the top to remove any excess chocolate and to level the surface.

• Gently place the dried strawberries onto the chocolate slab and sprinkle with the pink peppercorns. Leave to set in a cool dry place for at least 4 hours or overnight.

• Slowly loosen the chocolate from the moulds. Store in a cool dry place for up to a week.

Rice Bubbles Slab
with Honeycomb & Cranberries

preparation time : 30 minutes, plus setting
cook time : none

Vegetable oil for oiling
50 g (1¾ oz) Honeycomb (page 26)
30 g (1 oz) dried cranberries
20 g (¾ oz/⅔ cup) rice bubbles (rice crispies)
350 g (12½ oz) milk chocolate, tempered (see pages 126–9)

makes 2 *slabs*

- Lightly oil and line the base of two 15 × 10 cm (6 × 4 in) baking tins with baking paper, leaving some paper to overhang the sides for easy removal of the chocolate later.
- Chop the honeycomb into small pieces and mix in a bowl together with the cranberries and rice bubbles.
- Pour the chocolate onto the honeycomb mix and stir until everything is fully coated with the chocolate. Spoon the mixture into the prepared tins and leave to set in a cool dry place for at least 4 hours.
- Once set, lift out of the tins. Store in a cool dry place for up to a week.

9

Marzipan

Basic Marzipan

preparation time : 5 minutes
cook time : none

200 g (7 oz/2 cups) ground almonds

200 g (7 oz) icing (confectioners') sugar, plus extra for dusting

2 tablespoons liquid glucose

50 ml (1¾ fl oz) boiled water

½ teaspoon almond extract

A selection of food colourings (optional)

makes
450 g
(1 lb)

• Place the ground almonds and icing sugar in a food processor and pulse for a few seconds. Add the liquid glucose, boiled water and almond extract and continue to pulse until the mixture comes together.

• Lightly dust the work surface with icing sugar and knead the marzipan until smooth and pliable.

• The marzipan is now ready to use for covering fruitcakes and can be coloured and made into fruit shapes etc. Store in an airtight container for 3–4 weeks.

Pistachio Marzipan

Chocolates

preparation time : 30 minutes, plus drying and setting
cook time : none

TOOLS:

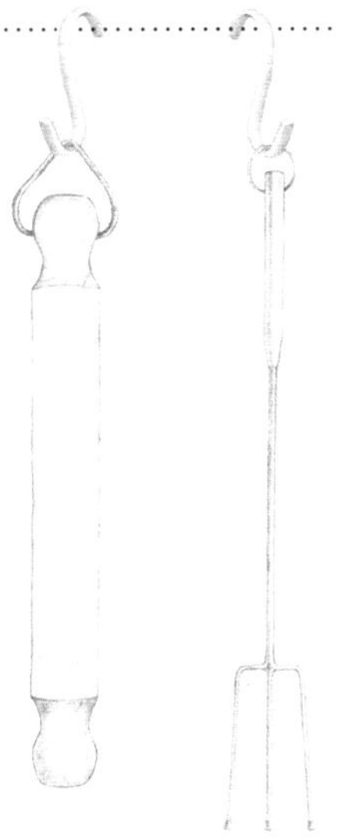

2 teaspoons sunflower oil, plus extra for oiling

100 g (3½ oz/⅔ cup) pistachio nuts, plus extra to decorate

Icing (confectioners') sugar for dusting

1 batch of Basic marzipan, about 450 g (1 lb) (page 190)

500 g (1 lb 2 oz) dark chocolate (at least 70% cocoa solids), tempered (see pages 126–9)

makes 40 *pieces*

• Lightly oil and line 2 baking trays with baking paper.

• Make pistachio paste by blitzing the oil and pistachio nuts in a food processor until smooth.

• Lightly dust a work surface with icing sugar and knead the plain marzipan. Add the pistachio paste and knead well for 5 minutes, or until it has been completely combined.

• Lightly dust the work surface with more icing sugar and roll out the marzipan into a rectangle about 1 cm (½ in) thick. Trim the sides of the rectangle, place onto the prepared tray and leave to dry for 10 minutes.

• Cut the marzipan into squares or shapes as desired, then dip the marzipan pieces into the tempered chocolate using dipping forks (see page 132). Shake off any excess chocolate and place on the other prepared baking tray.

• Decorate the marzipan with extra pistachio nuts and leave to set at room temperature for at least 2 hours. Store the chocolates in a cool, dry, dark place for up to a week.

10

Meringues

How To Make

Cold Meringue

1 Place 2 egg whites with a pinch of salt in a freestanding food mixer. Ensure that the bowl is clean and grease-free.

2 Attach a whisk to the mixer and whisk the egg whites on medium speed until they become frothy and start to form soft peaks.

3 Increase the speed to high and add 110 g (4 oz) caster (superfine) sugar, 1 tablespoon at a time, until all the sugar is used up.

4 The meringue should be smooth, glossy and holding stiff peaks.

5 With a metal spoon, fold in ⅛ teaspoon cream of tartar.

6 The meringue is now ready to use and can be baked in a low oven at 100°C (210°F).

1

2

3

4

5

6

How To Make

Italian Meringue

1 Combine 200 g (7 oz) caster (superfine) sugar, 1 tablespoon liquid glucose and 2 tablespoons water in a saucepan.

2 Heat over a medium heat, bring to the boil, insert a sugar thermometer and bring the syrup to 120°C (248°F).

3 Place 3 medium egg whites with a pinch of salt in a freestanding food mixer. Ensure that the bowl is clean and grease-free. Attach a whisk to the machine and start whisking the egg whites on medium speed.

4 Whisk until the egg whites become frothy and start to form soft peaks.

5 Increase the speed to high and slowly pour in the sugar syrup in a thin stream, whisking all the time until the syrup is used.

6 The meringue should be smooth, glossy, holding stiff peaks and looking like marshmallow. This meringue can be used to make bombe alaska, which does not require any cooking, and then finished with a blow torch to give it a nice caramelised colour.

1
2
3
4
5
6

Meringue Kisses

preparation time : 15 minutes
cook time : 1 hour, plus cooling

TOOLS:

2 egg whites
Pinch of salt
110 g (4 oz) caster (superfine) sugar
⅛ teaspoon cream of tartar
2 drops of food colouring as desired

makes
50–60
pieces

• Preheat the oven to 100°C (212°F). Line a large baking tray with baking paper.

• Place the egg whites and salt in a freestanding mixer with a whisk attachment. Make sure that the bowl is grease-free. Whisk the egg whites on medium speed until they become frothy and start to form soft peaks. Increase the speed to high and add tablespoonfuls of caster sugar, one spoonful at a time, until all the sugar is used up. The meringue should be smooth, glossy and holding stiff peaks. Remove the bowl from the mixer and, using a large metal spoon, stir in the cream of tartar and food colouring.

• Fill a piping bag with a star nozzle with the meringue mixture and pipe little kisses onto the prepared baking tray. Bake in the oven for 1 hour until dried and crisp.

• Leave to cool completely on a wire rack before removing from the baking tray. These meringue kisses can be stored in an airtight container for up to a week.

Meringue Logs
with Coffee & Hazelnut

preparation time : 15 minutes
cook time : 1–1½ hours, plus cooling

Vegetable oil for oiling
175 g (6 oz) caster (superfine) sugar
1 teaspoon instant espresso powder
3 egg whites
Pinch of salt
⅛ teaspoon cream of tartar
50 g (1¾ oz) whole blanched hazelnuts, toasted and chopped

100 g (3½ oz) dark chocolate (at least 70% cocoa solids), melted (optional)

TOOLS:

makes 8 *logs*

• Preheat the oven to 100°C (212°F). Lightly oil and line a large baking tray with baking paper.

• Mix the sugar and espresso powder in a small bowl and set aside.

• Place the egg whites and salt in a freestanding mixer with a whisk attachment. Make sure that the bowl is grease-free. Whisk the egg whites on medium speed until they become frothy and start to form soft peaks. Increase the speed to high and add tablespoonfuls of the sugar and espresso mixture, one spoonful at a time, until all the mixture has been used up. The meringue should be smooth, glossy and holding stiff peaks.

• Remove the bowl from the mixer and, using a large metal spoon, fold in the cream of tartar and half of the chopped hazelnuts until well combined.

• Fill a piping bag with a large plain nozzle with the meringue mixture and pipe 10–12 cm (4–4¾ in) logs onto the prepared baking tray. Sprinkle with the remaining nuts. Bake the meringues in the oven for 1–1½ hours, or until dried and crisp. Leave to cool completely on a wire rack before removing from the baking tray.

• Once cooled, drizzle some melted chocolate over the logs, if you like. The meringues can be stored in an airtight container for up to a week.

Chocolate Mushroom Meringues

preparation time : 20 minutes
cook time : 1–1½ hours, plus cooling and setting

Vegetable oil for oiling
250 g (9 oz) caster (superfine) sugar
5 g (¼ oz) unsweetened (Dutch) cocoa powder
3 egg whites
Pinch of salt
⅛ teaspoon cream of tartar

TOOLS:

100 g (3½ oz) dark chocolate (at least 70% cocoa solids), melted and tempered (see pages 126–9)
4 tablespoons sugar sprinkles

makes
15
mushrooms

• Preheat the oven to 100°C (212°F). Lightly oil and line 2 large baking trays with baking paper.

• Mix the caster sugar and cocoa powder together and set aside.

• Place the egg whites and salt in a freestanding mixer with a whisk attachment. Make sure that the bowl is grease-free. Whisk the egg whites on a medium speed until they become frothy and start to form soft peaks. Increase the speed to high and add tablespoonfuls of the caster sugar/cocoa mixture, one spoonful at a time, until all the mixture is used up. The meringue should be smooth, glossy and holding stiff peaks. Remove the bowl from the mixer and, using a large metal spoon, stir in the cream of tartar.

• Fill a piping bag with a large plain nozzle with the meringue mixture and pipe blobs, pulling the piping bag upwards to make spiky stems onto one of the prepared baking trays. On the other baking tray, pipe slightly larger blobs resembling domes.

• Bake the meringues in the oven for 1–1½ hours, or until dried and crisp. Leave to cool completely on a wire rack before removing from the baking tray.

• Once cool, make small holes in the bottoms of the domed meringues. Dip the tops of the dome-shaped meringues in the dark chocolate and sprinkle with sugar sprinkles. Leave to set at room temperature for 20 minutes. Gently place the dome-shaped meringues onto the spiky meringues to resemble mushrooms. Store in an airtight container for a week.

Raspberry Meringue Swirls

preparation time : 15 minutes
cook time : 1–1½ hours, plus cooling

TOOLS:

Vegetable oil for oiling
3 egg whites
Pinch of salt
175 g (6 oz) caster (superfine) sugar
⅛ teaspoon cream of tartar
½ teaspoon raspberry oil flavouring
Tiny amount of pink colouring paste
3 tablespoons freeze-dried raspberries

makes
6
meringues

• Preheat the oven to 100°C (212°F). Lightly oil and line a large baking tray with baking paper.

• Place the egg whites and salt in a freestanding mixer with a whisk attachment. Make sure the bowl is grease-free. Whisk on medium speed until they become frothy and start to form soft peaks. Increase the speed to high and add tablespoonfuls of caster sugar, one spoonful at a time, until it is used up. The meringue should be smooth, glossy and holding stiff peaks. Remove the bowl from the mixer and, using a large metal spoon, fold in the cream of tartar and the flavouring and colouring, stirring gently to give a marble effect.

• Place spoonfuls of the meringue onto the prepared baking tray, sprinkle over the freeze-dried raspberries, then bake in the oven for 1–1½ hours, or until dried and crisp.

• Leave to cool completely on a wire rack before removing from the baking tray. Store in an airtight container for up to a week.

Walnut Whip

Italian Meringue & Chocolate

preparation time : 30 minutes
cook time : 15–20 minutes, plus setting

Vegetable oil for oiling
400 g (14 oz) dark chocolate (at least 70% cocoa solids), melted and tempered (see pages 126–9)
100 g (3½ oz/1 cup) walnut halves, plus extra chopped walnuts to decorate
200 g (7 oz) caster (superfine) sugar
1 tablespoon liquid glucose
2 tablespoons water
3 medium egg whites
Pinch of salt

TOOLS:

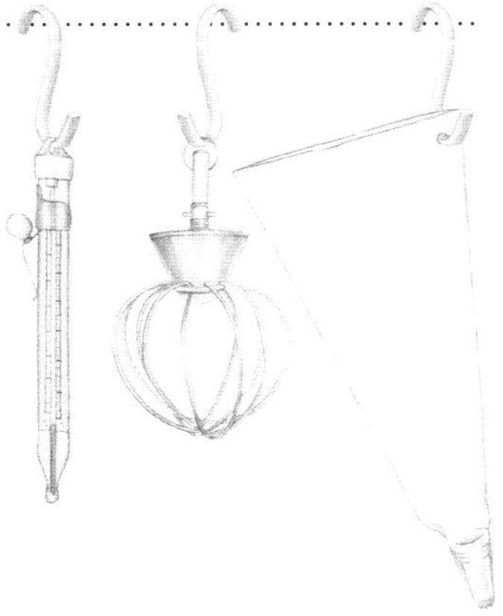

makes 20 *pieces*

• Lightly oil and line a baking tray with baking paper. Spoon some chocolate onto the prepared baking tray making 4 cm (1½ in) discs. Leave to set in a cool dry place for about 2 hours.

• In a frying pan, lightly toast the walnut halves and leave to cool.

• Bring the sugar, liquid glucose and water to the boil in a saucepan over a medium heat. Insert a sugar thermometer and cook until the syrup reaches 120°C (248°F).

• Place the egg whites and salt in a freestanding mixer with a whisk attachment. Make sure that the bowl is grease-free. Whisk the egg whites on a medium speed until the egg whites become frothy and start to form soft peaks. Increase the speed to high and slowly pour in the sugar syrup in a thin steady stream, whisking all the time, until all the syrup has been mixed in. The meringue should be smooth, glossy, holding stiff peaks and looking like marshmallow.

• Fill a piping bag with a plain nozzle with the meringue.

• Peel away or loosen the chocolate discs from the baking paper, then place the toasted walnuts in the middle of the chocolate discs and pipe the meringue onto the chocolate discs in the shape of a bee's hive. Sprinkle over some chopped walnut and, if desired, use a blow torch to lightly caramelise the meringue nests. Eat the on the day of making.

Macarons

preparation time : 40–45 minutes
cook time : 15–20 minutes, plus cooling

TOOLS:

Vegetable oil for oiling
100 g (3½ oz/1 cup) ground almonds
100 g (3½ oz) icing (confectioners') sugar
3 medium egg whites
100 g (3½ oz) caster (superfine) sugar
2 drops of each food colouring (violet, pink and green)

makes
46
macarons

• Preheat the oven to 180°C (350°F). Lightly oil a macaron tin or lightly oil and line a large baking tray with baking paper. Draw 2.5 cm (1 in) circles on the paper as a guide.

• In a food processor, blitz the ground almonds and icing sugar together, then sift into a bowl and set aside.

• Place the egg whites in a freestanding mixer with a whisk attachment and whisk until foamy. Add tablespoonfuls of the caster sugar, one spoonful at a time, until the meringue is shiny and glossy. Fold in the ground almonds and icing sugar mixture until well combined, then divide the mixture into 3 bowls, add the food colouring and mix well.

• Fill disposable piping bags with the mixture, then snip the ends and pipe within the indentations of the tin or onto the prepared tray. Leave for 5–10 minutes so the meringue dries out and forms a skin.

• Place in the oven and immediately reduce the oven temperature to 150°C (300°F) and bake for 15–20 minutes. Remove from the oven and leave to cool. As soon as the mixture is cool enough to handle, remove from the tin and cool on a wire rack.

• Once cooled, sandwich the macarons together with your desired filling or use the lavender, matcha and strawberry ganache on page 142. Unfilled macarons can be wrapped and frozen for up to a month or in an airtight container for up to a week.

11

Brittles

How To Make

Dry Caramel

1 Heat the sugar in a wide heavy-based saucepan until it has dissolved.

2 The sugar will start to colour a pale caramel.

3 Move the pan around to get an even heat and continue to let the sugar cook until it becomes amber in colour. The sugar will become caramel when it has reached the temperature 160–177°C (320–351°F).

4 Remove from the heat and use straight away by adding other ingredients or slowly plunge the pan into a bowl of iced water to stop it from cooking any further.

1

2

3

4

Flaked Almond Brittle

or Praline

preparation time : 5 minutes
cook time : 15–20 minutes, plus cooling and setting

150 g (5½ oz/1⅔ cups) toasted flaked almonds
300 g (10½ oz) caster (superfine) sugar

TOOLS:

makes
450 g
(1 lb)

• Line a baking tray with a silicone mat and spread over the almonds.

• Heat the sugar in a heavy-based saucepan until the sugar has dissolved. The sugar will start to go a pale caramel colour. Move the pan around to get an even heat and continue to let the sugar cook until it becomes golden amber in colour.

• Pour the mixture onto the almonds, making sure it spreads evenly. Leave to set in a cool dry place.

• Once it has cooled and set, break into shards with a rolling pin. Store in an airtight container in a cool dry place for up to 2 weeks.

TO MAKE PRALINE PASTE

1 batch (450 g/1 lb) of flaked almond brittle/praline

• Break the brittle into pieces with a rolling pin and then blitz in a food processor until it becomes sandy and paste-like.

• This may be used as a topping or filling for chocolates and desserts. Store in an airtight container in a cool dry place for up to 2 weeks.

Coffee & Hazelnut Brittle

preparation time : 5 minutes
cook time : 15–20 minutes, plus cooling

TOOLS:

Vegetable oil for oiling
100 g (3½ oz) whole hazelnuts, toasted
200 g (7 oz) caster (superfine) sugar
1 teaspoon espresso powder

makes
300 g
(10½ oz)

• Line the base and sides of a 15 x 21 cm (6 x 8¼ in) rectangular tin with baking paper, then lightly oil and set aside.

• Roughly chop the hazelnuts and put into the prepared tin, spreading evenly. Heat the sugar and espresso powder in a heavy-based saucepan until the sugar has dissolved. The sugar will start to colour a pale caramel. Move the pan around to get an even heat and continue to let the sugar cook until it becomes a golden amber colour. Pour the caramel over the chopped hazelnuts.

• Leave to cool and set in a cool dry place. Score indentation lines to make rectangles or squares before the brittle sets completely.

• Once cooled, break into shards with a rolling pin or break into the shaped pieces. Store in an airtight container in a cool dry place for up to 2 weeks.

Peanut & Sesame Brittle

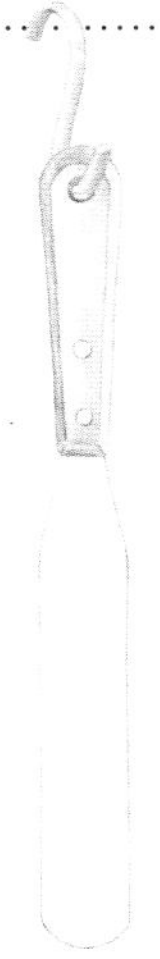

preparation time : 5–10 minutes
cook time : 15–20 minutes, plus cooling

TOOLS:

Vegetable oil for oiling
150 g (5½ oz) raw skinned peanuts
50 g (1¾ oz/⅓ cup) sesame seeds
300 g (10½ oz) caster (superfine) sugar

makes
500 g
(1 lb 2 oz)

• Line the base and sides of a 15 x 21 cm (6 x 8¼ in) rectangular tin with baking paper, then lightly oil and set aside.

• In a frying pan, lightly toast the peanuts, then remove from the pan and set aside.

• Lightly toast the sesame seeds in the same pan, then place in the prepared tin together with the peanuts.

• Heat the sugar in a heavy-based saucepan until the sugar has dissolved. The sugar will start to colour a pale caramel. Move the pan around to get an even heat and continue to let the sugar cook until it becomes a golden amber colour.

• Pour the caramel onto the nuts and seeds, ensuring they are covered evenly. Leave to cool slightly, then score rectangular lines on the brittle so it is easier to break into rectangle pieces. Store in an airtight container in a cool dry place for up to 2 weeks.

12

Sweet & Pretty

To Thread Stage

110–113°C

(230–235°F)

1 Place the sugar and water in a heavy-based saucepan.

2 Heat until the sugar has dissolved.

3 Place a sugar thermometer into the saucepan and boil the mixture.

4 If sugar is crystallising around the saucepan, clean around the saucepan with a damp pastry brush to prevent this.

5 Once the thermometer reaches the temperature, it has reached the thread stage.

6 To check it has reached this stage, drop a little of the sugar syrup into a bowl of cold water. The sugar will form a soft thread that does not keep its shape and dissolves away.

1

2

3

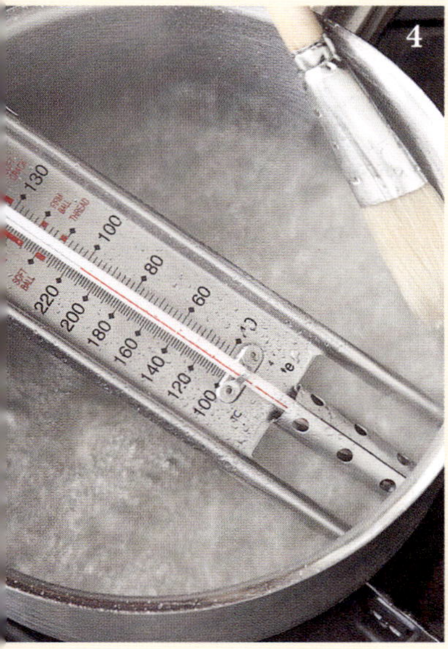
4

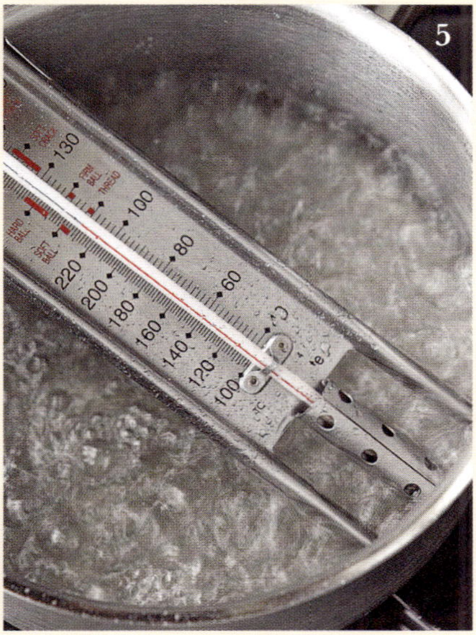
5

6

Rock Candy

preparation time : 5 minutes
cook time : 8–10 minutes, plus cooling and drying

TOOLS:

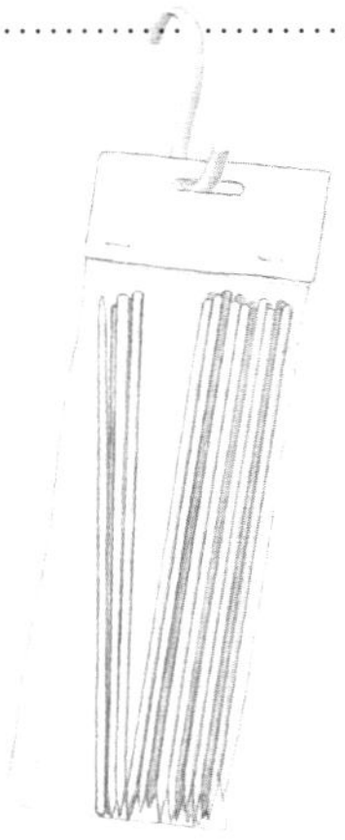

480 ml (16 fl oz) water
850 g (1 lb 14 oz) granulated sugar
Tiny amount of food colouring paste (pink, blue, green etc.) (optional)

makes
3 *large or* 6 *small*
bars

• Heat the water and 800 g (1 lb 12 oz) of the sugar in a saucepan until the sugar has dissolved and come to the boil, then gently boil for 2–3 minutes. Remove from the heat and leave the syrup until completely cool.

• Dip the skewers into the syrup for a few minutes until coated in the syrup then remove and roll in the remaining sugar. Let them dry out on baking paper overnight, or for up to 2 days in a dry place.

• Meanwhile, if desired, divide the syrup into different bowls and colour the syrup with food colouring of choice, mixing well.

• Place the coloured syrup into glasses and, once the skewers have dried, insert the skewers into the syrup suspended by securing with a clothes peg that rests over the glass tops. Leave for at least 7 days for crystals to grow onto the skewers. Keep an eye on the growth of the crystals daily to make sure that the bottom does not touch the glass.

• Once you are happy with the growth of crystals on the skewers, remove from the glass and leave to dry on baking paper. Store in an airtight container for up to a month.

Coloured Sugar Shapes

preparation time : 30 minutes, plus drying
cook time : none

TOOLS:

300 g ($10\frac{1}{2}$ oz) granulated sugar
2–4 tablespoons water
Tiny amount of food colouring pastes

makes
60–65
shapes

- Line baking trays with baking paper.
- Place the sugar and water in a bowl and mix well until you get a damp sandy texture.
- Divide the mixture into separate bowls to make different colours and add a small amount of food colouring paste to each bowl. Mix well, with a cocktail stick, until combined thoroughly.
- Tip the coloured sugars onto a clean board and press firmly with your hands to the depth of 1 cm ($\frac{1}{2}$ in) ensuring that the sugar is compact.
- Using different shaped cutters, cut out shapes and gently push out the sugar onto the prepared trays. Continue until all the sugar is used up. Leave to dry overnight in a cool dry place. Store in an airtight container in a cool dry place for up to a month.

Crystallised Flower Petals & Fruits

preparation time : 20–30 minutes, plus drying
cook time : none

2 egg whites
Pinch of salt
200 g (7 oz) caster (superfine) sugar
Selection of fruits: grapes, cherries, blueberries, strawberries, redcurrants etc.
Selection of edible flowers: rose petals, pansies or violets

TOOLS:

makes
30–40
pieces

• Line a baking tray with baking paper.

• Place the egg whites and salt in a small bowl and beat gently until slightly foamy.

• Place the sugar in a shallow bowl.

• Using a pastry brush, lightly brush the fruits and petals with some egg white, making sure that they are all covered in a thin layer, then dredge the fruits and petals in the sugar, making sure that they are completely coated. Shake off any excess sugar and place on the prepared baking tray. Leave to dry completely in a cool dry place for at least 3 hours.

• You can use these to decorate cakes. The crystallised flowers may be stored in an airtight container in a cool dry place for up to a week. The fruits will keep for up to 2–4 days.

Candied Orange Peel

preparation time : 20 minutes
cook time : 1 hour, plus cooling and drying

4 oranges
500 ml (17 fl oz/2 cups) water
500 g (1 lb 2 oz) granulated sugar

makes
250 g
(9 oz)

• Line a baking tray with baking paper.

• Using a sharp knife, cut quarter segments through the skin of the oranges and carefully peel off the skin, still keeping the quarter segment shapes intact. Remove any excess pith. Cut the segments into 1 cm (½ in) strips.

• Place the orange peels in a large saucepan and cover with cold water. Bring to the boil, then reduce the heat and simmer for 3–4 minutes. Drain the orange peels and repeat the process a couple more times, using fresh cold water, then drain the orange peels and set aside.

• Place the 500 ml (17 fl oz/2 cups) water and sugar in another large saucepan and place over the heat, stirring until the sugar has dissolved. Bring to the boil, then reduce the heat to a gentle simmer and add the blanched orange peel strips. Cook gently for about 1 hour, or until the orange peels become translucent and tender.

• Once tender, drain the peels thoroughly from the syrup and lay the strips in a single layer on the prepared baking tray. Leave the candied peel strips to dry in a cool dry place. This may take up to 2 days. Store in an airtight container for up to a month.

13

Re-creation of Chocolate Bars & Candy

Hazelnut, Wafer & Ganache

Chocolate Balls

preparation time : 55 minutes–1 hour, plus setting
cook time : none

TOOLS:

200 g (7 oz/6⅔ cups) rice bubbles (rice crispies), lightly crushed

1 batch of Basic dark chocolate ganache (page 134)

100 g (3½ oz) hazelnuts, chopped

500 g (1 lb 2 oz) milk chocolate, tempered (see pages 126–9)

makes
35–40
balls

• Line 2 baking trays with baking paper.

• Place the lightly crushed rice bubbles or crispies in a shallow dish or tray. Take teaspoonfuls of the ganache mix and roll into balls. Immediately roll into the crushed rice bubbles, pressing gently to coat and place on a prepared baking tray. Leave to set for 10 minutes.

• Stir the chopped hazelnuts into the chocolate and mix well.

• Dip the rice bubble coated ganache balls into the hazelnut chocolate mix, making sure that they are fully and evenly coated. Place on the other prepared baking tray and leave to set in a cool dry place for at least 2 hours. Store in an airtight container in a cool dry place for up to 5 days.

Chocolate Mint
Fondants

preparation time : 20–30 minutes
cook time : 15–20 minutes, plus cooling and setting

TOOLS:

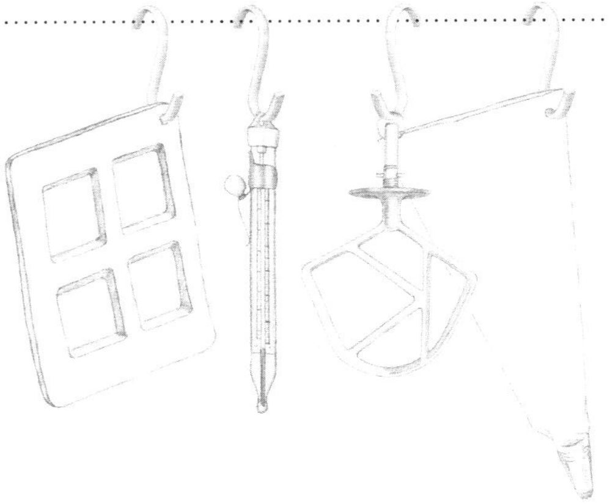

250 g (9 oz) dark chocolate, tempered (see pages 126–9)
200 g (7 oz) granulated sugar
60 ml (2 fl oz/¼ cup) water
1 tablespoon liquid glucose
25 g (1 oz) unsalted butter
1 teaspoon mint oil flavouring

makes
35–40
fondants

• Cover a silicone or plastic chocolate mould with the tempered chocolate and leave to set for 15–20 minutes (see page 130).

• Meanwhile, place the sugar, water and liquid glucose in a heavy-based saucepan. Place over a medium heat and stir until the sugar has dissolved. Insert a sugar thermometer and bring to the boil. Reduce the heat and simmer until the syrup reaches 121°C (250°F).

• Remove from the heat and add the butter and mint flavouring. Stir well to mix thoroughly. Place the mixture in a freestanding food mixer with a paddle attachment and beat on medium speed until the mixture thickens slightly and turns opaque.

• Once the mixture has cooled and thickened slightly, but is still runny, place into a piping bag and pipe into the chocolate moulds almost to the top. Leave to set for about 15 minutes then cover the fondants with more chocolate as described on page 130. Leave to set for at least 3–4 hours before unmoulding. Store in an airtight container for up to a week.

Coconut & Lime
Chocolate Bars

preparation time : 20 minutes
cook time : 10 minutes, plus cooling and setting

TOOLS:

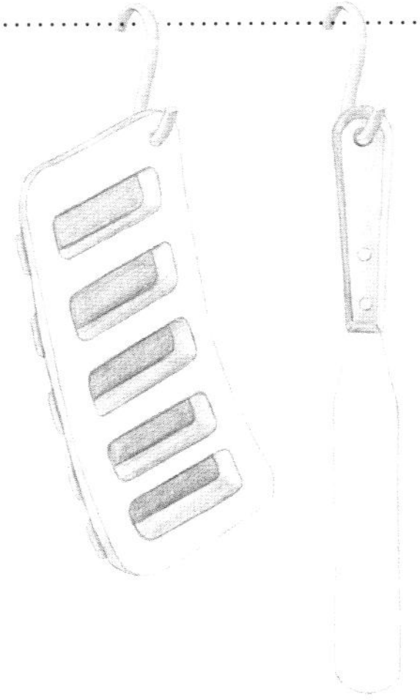

150 ml (5 fl oz) condensed milk
75 ml (2½ fl oz) liquid glucose
100 g (3½ oz) desiccated coconut
Juice and finely grated zest of 1 lime
500 g (1 lb 2 oz) dark chocolate (at least 70% cocoa solids), tempered (see pages 126–9)

makes
8
bars

• Place the condensed milk and liquid glucose in a saucepan. Place over a low heat and gently cook for 5 minutes until well combined. Stir in the desiccated coconut and lime juice and zest. Mix well and cook for a further 2 minutes. Remove from the heat, place in a bowl and leave to cool at room temperature.

• Cover a chocolate bar mould with the tempered chocolate (see page 130) and leave to set for 15–20 minutes.

• Once the chocolate has set, using a teaspoon, fill the cavity with the cooled coconut mixture until almost full, then pour more chocolate over to cover then leave to set for 3–4 hours before removing from the mould. Store in an airtight container in a cool dry place for up to a week.

Peanut & Caramel

Chocolate Bars

preparation time : 30–40 minutes
cook time : 10–15 minutes, plus cooling and setting

TOOLS:

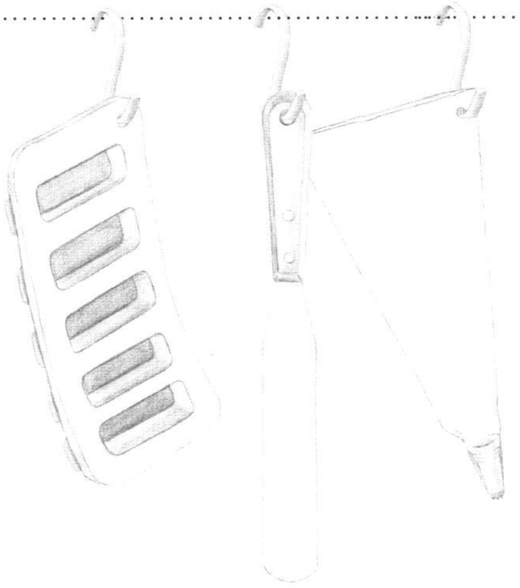

200 g (7 oz) raw skinned peanuts
500 g (1 lb 2 oz) milk chocolate, tempered (see pages 126–9)
½ batch of soft caramel filling (see page 168)
½ batch of Basic nougat (page 96), omitting the fruit and nuts
50 g (1¾ oz) milk chocolate, melted

makes 8 *bars*

- Preheat the oven to 180°C (350°F).
- Place the peanuts on a baking tray and roast in the oven for 10 minutes until golden brown. Remove from the oven and leave to cool. Roughly chop half of the peanuts and leave the rest whole.
- Cover a chocolate bar mould with the tempered chocolate (see page 130) and leave to set in a cool dry place for 15–20 minutes.
- Mix the soft caramel and peanuts together in a bowl.
- Once the chocolate bar mould has set, fill the cavity with the peanut and caramel mixture until half full, then leave to set for 10 minutes in a cool dry place.
- In a bowl, thoroughly mix the basic nougat mixture with the 50 g (1¾ oz) melted milk chocolate. Place in a disposable piping bag, snip off the end and pipe onto the set peanut caramels. Leave to set again in a cool dry place for 10 minutes.
- Cover the top of the nougat with more chocolate then leave to set for 3–4 hours before removing from the mould. Store in an airtight container in a cool dry place for up to a week.

Shortbread & Caramel

Chocolate Bars

preparation time : 20 minutes
cook time : 45–50 minutes, plus cooling, chilling and setting

TOOLS:

175 g (6 oz) unsalted butter

75 g ($2^3/_4$ oz) caster (superfine) sugar

225 g (8 oz/$1^1/_2$ cups) plain (all-purpose) flour

1 batch of soft caramel filling, about 400 g (14 oz) (see page 168)

500 g (1 lb 2 oz) milk chocolate, tempered (see pages 126–9)

makes
18
bars

• Preheat the oven to 160°C (320°F) and line the base and sides of a 19 cm ($7^1/_2$ in) square cake tin with baking paper, then oil and line a baking tray with baking paper.

• Put the butter, sugar and flour in a large bowl and rub together to make a dough. Press the dough into the prepared cake tin and prick all over with a fork.

• Make indentation lines on the dough of 9.5 x 2 cm ($3^3/_4$ x $^3/_4$ in) rectangles, then bake in the oven for 15–20 minutes. Remove from the oven and leave to cool on a wire rack.

• Meanwhile, put the caramel into a disposable piping bag and chill in the refrigerator until needed.

• Take the shortbread out of the tin and turn over onto a baking tray. With a palette knife spread some tempered chocolate over the shortbread until it is covered then leave to set in a cool dry place.

• Once set, turn over and cut into the rectangles. Remove the caramel from the refrigerator and pipe along the length of the shortbread. Put the shortbread caramels onto a wire rack with a tray underneath and pour ladlefuls of the chocolate over them. Let the chocolate drip down, tapping the wire rack on the tray. Gently lift the chocolate covered shortbread with a palette knife onto a baking tray and leave the chocolate to set in a cool dry place for at least 3–4 hours. Store in an airtight container in a cool dry place for up to a week.

Milk Candy

preparation time : 25–30 minutes
cook time : 20–30 minutes

TOOLS:

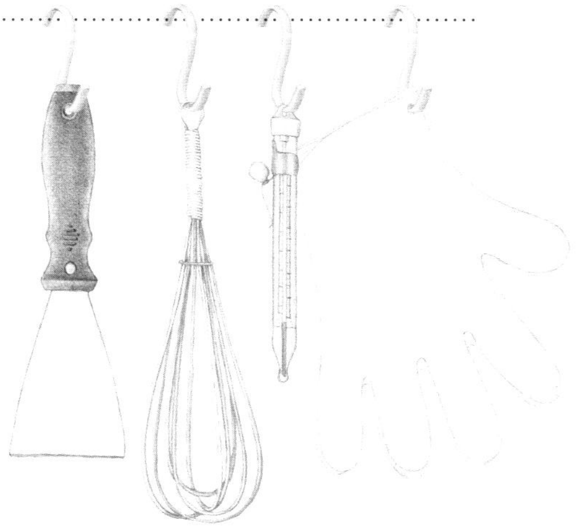

Vegetable oil for oiling
200 g (7 oz) granulated sugar
125 ml (4 fl oz/½ cup) liquid glucose
60 ml (2 fl oz/¼ cup) evaporated milk
60 ml (2 fl oz/¼ cup) condensed milk
15 g (½ oz) unsalted butter
1 teaspoon cornflour (cornstarch)
1 teaspoon vanilla extract
Rice paper for wrapping

makes
40
pieces

• Lightly oil a marble slab or a silicone mat and a metal scraper or palette knives.

• Place the sugar, liquid glucose, evaporated milk, condensed milk, butter and cornflour into a pan. Place over a low heat and whisk the mixture until smooth, then with a wooden spoon stir the sugar until dissolved. Increase the heat, insert a sugar thermometer and cook until the mixture reaches 121°C (250°F). The mixture should become a light caramel colour.

• Remove from the heat and carefully pour the syrup onto the oiled marble slab or silicone mat. As the syrup is runny at this stage, work quickly. Use the metal scraper to gently push or scrape the outer edges of the sugar inwards to the middle. Keep doing this until the syrup starts to cool down and thicken. Add the vanilla extract and mix well.

• Once the syrup is cool enough to handle, put on some latex gloves and lightly oil them. Start pulling the now thickened syrup, bringing the ends together. Pull and bring the ends back together as this aerates the syrup and makes it chewy. Repeat this until it is difficult to pull anymore. The mixture should now be a lighter creamy shade of colour and still pliable.

• Divide the mixture in half, lightly oil the marble slab again and roll the chewy candy to a diameter thickness of 5 mm (¼ in). Using the metal scraper, cut the candy into 2.5 cm (1 in) lengths.

• Wrap the candy individually in the rice paper then wrap in cellophane or greaseproof (wax) paper. Store in an airtight container in a cool dry place for up to a week.

Index

Acknowledgements

Life is sweet … so cherish it.

I would like to dedicate this book to my mum, Kathleen Muna, and my dad, Othman, for all their love and support through this journey. To my sisters, Rosina, Jelita and my brothers Jaffery and Amin, a big thanks for being there and for all your support. Thank you to Janet Reeve, Michaella Pentucci and Poppy Campbell for your hard work and help on the photo shoot. You've been great girls!

I would like to say a huge thank you to Lisa Linder for the amazing photos; Catie Ziller and Kathy Steer for their brilliant editorial work and Alice Chadwick for her great designs and illustrations. Not forgetting the French team too, merci! Thank you all for this wonderful experience and for this book.

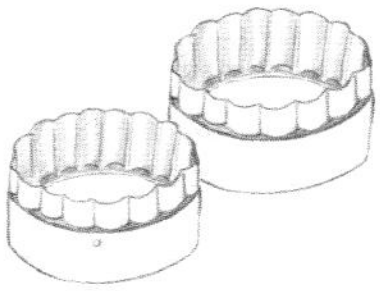

This edition published by Hardie Grant Books in 2015

First published by Hachette Livre (Marabout) in 2013

Hardie Grant Books (Australia)
Ground Floor, Building 1, 658 Church Street
Richmond, Victoria 3121
www.hardiegrant.com.au

Hardie Grant Books (UK)
5th & 6th Floor, 52–54 Southwark Street
London SE1 1RU
www.hardiegrant.co.uk

Design and illustration: Alice Chadwick
Photography: Lisa Linder

ISBN: 9781742708683

Colour reproduction by Splitting Image Colour Studio
Printed and bound in China by 1010 Printing International Limited